Stay connected. Stay playful. Stay loving. Stay excited. Stay healthy. Stay supportive. Stay visionary. Stay collaborative. Stay vibrant. Stay alive. Stay motivated. Stay curious. Stay grounded. Stay compassionate. Stay wise. Stay _____. Stay resilient. Stay _____. Stay resourceful. Stay _____. Stay inspiring. Stay _____ innovative. Stay persis_____. Stay courageou_____ funny. Stay clea_____. Stay determined. Stay creative. Stay ethical. Stay confident. Stay adaptable. Stay resolute. Stay easeful. Stay aware. Stay attuned. Stay organized. Stay approachable. Stay open-minded. Stay perceptive. Stay mindful. Stay energized. Stay engaged. Stay prepared. Stay rooted. Stay encouraging. Stay hopeful. Stay goofy. Stay inspired. Stay exacting. Stay proud. Stay steady. Stay joyful. Stay bold. Stay aligned. Stay yourself.

Planner to Stay

Learning Humans

Planner to Stay: An Annual Calendar for Refueling, Remoralizing, and Reclamation

Published by Learning Humans Press, Salt Lake City, UT, USA. Distributed globally in English with Expanded Distribution by IngramSpark and KDP.

ISBN Paperback: 979-8-9880470-2-5
Library of Congress Control Number: 2025918096

 Learning Humans

For more information, please visit www.jesscleeves.com.

Planner to Stay

An Annual Calendar

for Refueling, Remoralizing, and Reclamation

Jess Cleeves, MAT, LCSW

 Learning Humans

Dear Educator –

I'm so glad you're here.

By here, I mean here, thinking about how to make your practice survivable, sustainable, and meaningful. I mean, here, near or in a classroom - or not. I mean, here, in your body , on this planet, with your heart beating in your chest and your mind firing in a pattern that has never existed before in the history of the universe - and that will never exist again.

I'm so glad you're here, because you are essential.

I don't necessarily know you, specifically - but I don't actually need to. By virtue of your choice to teach, I know enough about you to know that you care deeply about your world and about the learners you are supporting, and that you are visionary enough to understand that you are supporting those learners to shape and care for that world long after you have left it. It's amazing that you are motivated by such care. You are amazing.

You are also vulnerable. The same generosity that drives you to build a career in the service of the greater good also makes you susceptible to giving of yourself at rates and quantities that range from unsustainable to unsurvivable.

This planner is a tool to support you to stay connected to yourself, your agency, your power, your heart, and your values as you stay connected to work you (want to) love. You can use this planner as a stand-alone support. You may get more out of this planner if you read its namesake book *Planning to Stay: Burnout, Demoralization, Exploitation, and How to Reclaim Self- Care, Your Classroom, and Your Life… Anyway*, and if you're able to engage in the companion *Planning to Stay Workbook*.

However you found this planner, I sincerely hope it helps you to find yourself in your practice every day.

In loving solidarity,

jess

Learning Humans

Table of Contents

How to Use This Planner

1. Independently or With Support

This planner was set up based on the book *Planning to Stay: Burnout, Demoralization, Exploitation, and How to Reclaim Self-Care, Your Classroom, and Your Life... Anyway.* If you have read the book, the ideas in this planner may make more sense to you than if you haven't read it yet. That said, all of the activities in this planner are also useful on their own.

If you'd prefer a spiral-bound version, easy! Just take this book to your nearest printing store or district publishing center and ask them to slice off the binding and thread a coil through for you.

2. At a Pace That Works for You

Each page of this planner contains many ideas and invitations. You are not responsible for "completing" anything. You can use it one day, put it down for a month, and then use it again when it feels available to you.

The first few pages include information that will help you to better utilize the monthly and weekly sections. Consider reading through the supporting material contained in pages 13-43 to orient yourself as you decide how you'd like to utilize the rest.

3. As An Act of Care

This empty book is ready to be filled with your care - care for your community, for the learners you support, and, most certainly, care for yourself. It is not a list of tasks or demands - it starts blank, but it starts full. You can only add to it, and you can't fail. Every time you engage with your planner, your engagement counts as an act of care.

Learning Humans

Defining Burnout, Demoralization, and Exploitation

Burnout

Burnout is a simple equation; energy out > energy in. It occurs when the energy we have available for a given task or idea is less than the energy the task or idea requires. Of the three causes of professional discontent (burnout, demoralization, and exploitation), burnout is the easiest to identify, the quickest to remedy, and the speediest to heal after behavior change. We'll be grateful for burnout's reference to flame as a pneumonic device, as fuel is shorthand for stored energy. Over short periods, we can usually recover from energy discrepancies. For example, we may be exhausted after organizing community members as audience members for student presentations on a Friday, but if we can rest over the weekend and return enthusiastically, our overall energetic balance doesn't tip towards burnout. If, however, tiny daily imbalances don't have the chance to refresh over time, we'll experience the numb exhaustion characteristic of burnout.

Intentional Refueling

Heal burnout by focusing on the tasks that fuel you, and increasing your efficiency at handling/limiting those that don't. In general, refueling happens when we tune in to key self-care categories. These categories will be referenced throughout the planner:

 **Intellectual:** anything that gets you wondering or interested in ideas

 Physical: moving and/or feeling your body in any way

 **Social:** connecting with other adults about anything, ideally not work

 Emotional: naming and feeling your own feelings

 **Spiritual:** connecting with something greater than yourself

Defining Burnout, Demoralization, and Exploitation

Demoralization

"Demoralization" was coined by Dr. Doris Santoro, who distinguished demoralization as a separate phenomenon from burnout. Demoralization occurs when the values we are asked to enact in our day to day teaching practice are different from, or in opposition to, the values that true us to the work in the first place. Working to heal demoralization is a tricky task for many teachers, as it requires us to hold multiple truths at the same time: the overall system may not support the values we wish to enact in our classroom every day, but we can still find ways to connect with and embody our own values, anyway. This insistence requires discipline, and a commitment to focus on our own motivating values. This planner will support you to do that work, as its pages are perpetually peppered with opportunities to re-affirm the values you'd like to motivate your practice.

Heal demoralization by acknowledging the difference between the values that motivate your practice and that infuse your daily demands, and intentionally build opportunities to enact your values in your day-to-day practice.

Exploitation

Exploitation is the inevitable interaction of the giving nature of educators as helpers and the taking nature of the system in which they work. When educators are experiencing exploitation, it often sounds and feels personal, but it's actually not personal at all. We take being exploited personally because we confuse our availability for caring relationships with our students and community with a caring relationship to our entire job on balance. By understanding that you are not in relationship with the system, you can navigate it like you do other unwieldy, potentially harmful structures. The U.S. public education system is built to extract from educators maximally. It's up to us, teacher by teacher, to draw boundaries to protect ourselves, and to do our own personal work to validate that all we give is, indeed, enough.

Heal exploitation by adhering firmly to a clear contract of what you will - and will not - offer your practice by setting clear, positive boundaries.

Diagnosing Burnout, Demoralization, and Exploitation

Check any of the statements that apply to you and your teaching practice during the school year. Re-visit this list via the following multiple copies to track how your experience is evolving.

Burnout

- ☐ I rarely feel rested.
- ☐ I forget or mishandle my own important personal affairs (paying bills, registering vehicles, etc).
- ☐ I have little energy for my personal life after work.
- ☐ I don't care if it makes me a bad teacher, I leave at the end of my paid contract day whether I'm ready for the next school day or not.
- ☐ I do not exercise (I mean nothing—not even a walk around the block).
- ☐ I have difficulty falling asleep, and/or I wake up in the middle of the night with anxiety about all of the tasks I have yet to complete.
- ☐ I say 'no' to any extra asks without listening to or considering what the asks are.
- ☐ I speak to people that I love with sharpness or impatience that I'm not proud of.
- ☐ I frequently feel overwhelmed.
- ☐ I am so stressed about getting stuff done that I'm less efficient in actually getting stuff done.

Demoralization

- ☐ I am obligated to use scripted curricula, but I'd rather not.
- ☐ I am obligated to use a curriculum I dislike.
- ☐ I have little control over how my classroom time is spent.
- ☐ I am unable to sufficiently respond to my students who need help, both in and out of the classroom.
- ☐ I am concerned about the harm that other colleagues in my school are causing to my students.
- ☐ I feel I am causing my students harm with the pedagogy/testing I am required to facilitate.
- ☐ I carry negative feelings about students whose performance may negatively impact my data.
- ☐ I am evaluated on practices that I don't believe are the most impactful for student outcomes.
- ☐ I am critiqued without suggestions for improvement or acknowledgment of what I do well.
- ☐ It's hard for me to focus on my teaching because of all of the forms, meetings, activities, and additional responsibilities expected of me by my school/district/state.

Exploitation

- ☐ I spend most of Sunday dreading Monday.
- ☐ I feel anxious about my professional relationships with colleagues and administrators.
- ☐ When parents complain, administrators rarely defend or support me.
- ☐ I spend personal money and time on school-related materials.
- ☐ I no longer attempt to contribute ideas during professional meetings because it's unsafe to do so, and my ideas aren't considered.
- ☐ I am constantly aware of how I could be doing things better, and that awareness causes me stress.
- ☐ I am not supported by my administration in school policy enforcement.
- ☐ There are multiple examples of unequal resource distribution among teachers in my school.
- ☐ My administrators have "favorite" educators who receive more support than other educators.
- ☐ I am expected (explicitly or implicitly) to volunteer for after-school support, or other school-related activities.

Prescription

Tally your scores: **Burnout:** /10   **Demoralization:** /10   **Exploitation:** /10

Use your relative scores to determine which phenomena may be more or less impactful to your practice. Use this information to tailor your self-care as you continue through the book.

☙ Learning Humans

Diagnosing Burnout, Demoralization, and Exploitation

Check any of the statements that apply to you and your teaching practice during the school year. Re-visit this list via the following multiple copies to track how your experience is evolving.

Burnout

☐ I rarely feel rested.

☐ I forget or mishandle my own important personal affairs (paying bills, registering vehicles, etc).

☐ I have little energy for my personal life after work.

☐ I don't care if it makes me a bad teacher, I leave at the end of my paid contract day whether I'm ready for the next school day or not.

☐ I do not exercise (I mean nothing—not even a walk around the block).

☐ I have difficulty falling asleep, and/or I wake up in the middle of the night with anxiety about all of the tasks I have yet to complete.

☐ I say 'no' to any extra asks without listening to or considering what the asks are.

☐ I speak to people that I love with sharpness or impatience that I'm not proud of.

☐ I frequently feel overwhelmed.

☐ I am so stressed about getting stuff done that I'm less efficient in actually getting stuff done.

Demoralization

☐ I am obligated to use scripted curricula, but I'd rather not.

☐ I am obligated to use a curriculum I dislike.

☐ I have little control over how my classroom time is spent.

☐ I am unable to sufficiently respond to my students who need help, both in and out of the classroom.

☐ I am concerned about the harm that other colleagues in my school are causing to my students.

☐ I feel I am causing my students harm with the pedagogy/testing I am required to facilitate.

☐ I carry negative feelings about students whose performance may negatively impact my data.

☐ I am evaluated on practices that I don't believe are the most impactful for student outcomes.

☐ I am critiqued without suggestions for improvement or acknowledgment of what I do well.

☐ It's hard for me to focus on my teaching because of all of the forms, meetings, activities, and additional responsibilities expected of me by my school/district/state.

Exploitation

☐ I spend most of Sunday dreading Monday.

☐ I feel anxious about my professional relationships with colleagues and administrators.

☐ When parents complain, administrators rarely defend or support me.

☐ I spend personal money and time on school-related materials.

☐ I no longer attempt to contribute ideas during professional meetings because it's unsafe to do so, and my ideas aren't considered.

☐ I am constantly aware of how I could be doing things better, and that awareness causes me stress.

☐ I am not supported by my administration in school policy enforcement.

☐ There are multiple examples of unequal resource distribution among teachers in my school.

☐ My administrators have "favorite" educators who receive more support than other educators.

☐ I am expected (explicitly or implicitly) to volunteer for after-school support, or other school-related activities.

Prescription

Tally your scores: **Burnout:** /10   **Demoralization:** /10   **Exploitation:** /10

Use your relative scores to determine which phenomena may be more or less impactful to your practice. Use this information to tailor your self-care as you continue through the book.

🧠 Learning Humans

Diagnosing Burnout, Demoralization, and Exploitation

Check any of the statements that apply to you and your teaching practice during the school year. Re-visit this list via the following multiple copies to track how your experience is evolving.

Burnout

- ☐ I rarely feel rested.
- ☐ I forget or mishandle my own important personal affairs (paying bills, registering vehicles, etc).
- ☐ I have little energy for my personal life after work.
- ☐ I don't care if it makes me a bad teacher, I leave at the end of my paid contract day whether I'm ready for the next school day or not.
- ☐ I do not exercise (I mean nothing—not even a walk around the block).
- ☐ I have difficulty falling asleep, and/or I wake up in the middle of the night with anxiety about all of the tasks I have yet to complete.
- ☐ I say 'no' to any extra asks without listening to or considering what the asks are.
- ☐ I speak to people that I love with sharpness or impatience that I'm not proud of.
- ☐ I frequently feel overwhelmed.
- ☐ I am so stressed about getting stuff done that I'm less efficient in actually getting stuff done.

Demoralization

- ☐ I am obligated to use scripted curricula, but I'd rather not.
- ☐ I am obligated to use a curriculum I dislike.
- ☐ I have little control over how my classroom time is spent.
- ☐ I am unable to sufficiently respond to my students who need help, both in and out of the classroom.
- ☐ I am concerned about the harm that other colleagues in my school are causing to my students.
- ☐ I feel I am causing my students harm with the pedagogy/testing I am required to facilitate.
- ☐ I carry negative feelings about students whose performance may negatively impact my data.
- ☐ I am evaluated on practices that I don't believe are the most impactful for student outcomes.
- ☐ I am critiqued without suggestions for improvement or acknowledgment of what I do well.
- ☐ It's hard for me to focus on my teaching because of all of the forms, meetings, activities, and additional responsibilities expected of me by my school/district/state.

Exploitation

- ☐ I spend most of Sunday dreading Monday.
- ☐ I feel anxious about my professional relationships with colleagues and administrators.
- ☐ When parents complain, administrators rarely defend or support me.
- ☐ I spend personal money and time on school-related materials.
- ☐ I no longer attempt to contribute ideas during professional meetings because it's unsafe to do so, and my ideas aren't considered.
- ☐ I am constantly aware of how I could be doing things better, and that awareness causes me stress.
- ☐ I am not supported by my administration in school policy enforcement.
- ☐ There are multiple examples of unequal resource distribution among teachers in my school.
- ☐ My administrators have "favorite" educators who receive more support than other educators.
- ☐ I am expected (explicitly or implicitly) to volunteer for after-school support, or other school-related activities.

Prescription

Tally your scores: **Burnout:** /10   **Demoralization:** /10   **Exploitation:** /10

Use your relative scores to determine which phenomena may be more or less impactful to your practice. Use this information to tailor your self-care as you continue through the book.

 Learning Humans

Diagnosing Burnout, Demoralization, and Exploitation

Check any of the statements that apply to you and your teaching practice during the school year. Re-visit this list via the following multiple copies to track how your experience is evolving.

Burnout

- [ ] I rarely feel rested.
- [ ] I forget or mishandle my own important personal affairs (paying bills, registering vehicles, etc).
- [ ] I have little energy for my personal life after work.
- [ ] I don't care if it makes me a bad teacher, I leave at the end of my paid contract day whether I'm ready for the next school day or not.
- [ ] I do not exercise (I mean nothing—not even a walk around the block).
- [ ] I have difficulty falling asleep, and/or I wake up in the middle of the night with anxiety about all of the tasks I have yet to complete.
- [ ] I say 'no' to any extra asks without listening to or considering what the asks are.
- [ ] I speak to people that I love with sharpness or impatience that I'm not proud of.
- [ ] I frequently feel overwhelmed.
- [ ] I am so stressed about getting stuff done that I'm less efficient in actually getting stuff done.

Demoralization

- [ ] I am obligated to use scripted curricula, but I'd rather not.
- [ ] I am obligated to use a curriculum I dislike.
- [ ] I have little control over how my classroom time is spent.
- [ ] I am unable to sufficiently respond to my students who need help, both in and out of the classroom.
- [ ] I am concerned about the harm that other colleagues in my school are causing to my students.
- [ ] I feel I am causing my students harm with the pedagogy/testing I am required to facilitate.
- [ ] I carry negative feelings about students whose performance may negatively impact my data.
- [ ] I am evaluated on practices that I don't believe are the most impactful for student outcomes.
- [ ] I am critiqued without suggestions for improvement or acknowledgment of what I do well.
- [ ] It's hard for me to focus on my teaching because of all of the forms, meetings, activities, and additional responsibilities expected of me by my school/district/state.

Exploitation

- [ ] I spend most of Sunday dreading Monday.
- [ ] I feel anxious about my professional relationships with colleagues and administrators.
- [ ] When parents complain, administrators rarely defend or support me.
- [ ] I spend personal money and time on school-related materials.
- [ ] I no longer attempt to contribute ideas during professional meetings because it's unsafe to do so, and my ideas aren't considered.
- [ ] I am constantly aware of how I could be doing things better, and that awareness causes me stress.
- [ ] I am not supported by my administration in school policy enforcement.
- [ ] There are multiple examples of unequal resource distribution among teachers in my school.
- [ ] My administrators have "favorite" educators who receive more support than other educators.
- [ ] I am expected (explicitly or implicitly) to volunteer for after-school support, or other school-related activities.

Prescription

Tally your scores: **Burnout:** /10   **Demoralization:** /10   **Exploitation:** /10

Use your relative scores to determine which phenomena may be more or less impactful to your practice. Use this information to tailor your self-care as you continue through the book.

Learning Humans

Diagnosing Burnout, Demoralization, and Exploitation

Check any of the statements that apply to you and your teaching practice during the school year. Re-visit this list via the following multiple copies to track how your experience is evolving.

Burnout

- ☐ I rarely feel rested.
- ☐ I forget or mishandle my own important personal affairs (paying bills, registering vehicles, etc).
- ☐ I have little energy for my personal life after work.
- ☐ I don't care if it makes me a bad teacher, I leave at the end of my paid contract day whether I'm ready for the next school day or not.
- ☐ I do not exercise (I mean nothing—not even a walk around the block).
- ☐ I have difficulty falling asleep, and/or I wake up in the middle of the night with anxiety about all of the tasks I have yet to complete.
- ☐ I say 'no' to any extra asks without listening to or considering what the asks are.
- ☐ I speak to people that I love with sharpness or impatience that I'm not proud of.
- ☐ I frequently feel overwhelmed.
- ☐ I am so stressed about getting stuff done that I'm less efficient in actually getting stuff done.

Demoralization

- ☐ I am obligated to use scripted curricula, but I'd rather not.
- ☐ I am obligated to use a curriculum I dislike.
- ☐ I have little control over how my classroom time is spent.
- ☐ I am unable to sufficiently respond to my students who need help, both in and out of the classroom.
- ☐ I am concerned about the harm that other colleagues in my school are causing to my students.
- ☐ I feel I am causing my students harm with the pedagogy/testing I am required to facilitate.
- ☐ I carry negative feelings about students whose performance may negatively impact my data.
- ☐ I am evaluated on practices that I don't believe are the most impactful for student outcomes.
- ☐ I am critiqued without suggestions for improvement or acknowledgment of what I do well.
- ☐ It's hard for me to focus on my teaching because of all of the forms, meetings, activities, and additional responsibilities expected of me by my school/district/state.

Exploitation

- ☐ I spend most of Sunday dreading Monday.
- ☐ I feel anxious about my professional relationships with colleagues and administrators.
- ☐ When parents complain, administrators rarely defend or support me.
- ☐ I spend personal money and time on school-related materials.
- ☐ I no longer attempt to contribute ideas during professional meetings because it's unsafe to do so, and my ideas aren't considered.
- ☐ I am constantly aware of how I could be doing things better, and that awareness causes me stress.
- ☐ I am not supported by my administration in school policy enforcement.
- ☐ There are multiple examples of unequal resource distribution among teachers in my school.
- ☐ My administrators have "favorite" educators who receive more support than other educators.
- ☐ I am expected (explicitly or implicitly) to volunteer for after-school support, or other school-related activities.

Prescription

Tally your scores: **Burnout: /10   Demoralization: /10   Exploitation: /10**

Use your relative scores to determine which phenomena may be more or less impactful to your practice. Use this information to tailor your self-care as you continue through the book.

 Learning Humans

Stay Connected to Your Values

Identify your values by marking them with these corresponding symbols:

Indicate	Identify your values for each of the following questions:
Check mark	What ✓values defined your family's relationship to work?
Underline	What <u>values</u> were prominent in the way you thought/acted when you were a student (think of yourself at the age/grade level that you teach)?
Asterisk	What .values drew you to teaching as a profession?
Question Mark	What . values define your current teaching practice (whether you want them to or not)?
Circle	What [values] do you WANT to define your teaching practice moving forward?

Acceptance	Commitment	Drive	Grace
Accomplishment	Communication	Effectiveness	Gratitude
Accountability	Community	Efficiency	Greatness
Accuracy	Compassion	Empathy	Growth
Achievement	Competence	Emotionality	Happiness
Adaptability	Concentration	Empowerment	Hard work
Alertness	Confidence	Endurance	Harmony
Altruism	Connection	Energy	Health
Ambition	Consciousness	Enjoyment	Honesty
Amusement	Consistency	Enthusiasm	Honor
Assertiveness	Contentment	Equality	Hope
Attunement	Contribution	Ethics	Humility
Awareness	Control	Excellence	Humor
Balance	Conviction	Experience	Imagination
Beauty	Cooperation	Exploration	Improvement
Boldness	Courage	Expression	Independence
Bravery	Courtesy	Fairness	Individuality
Brilliance	Creativity	Faith	Innovation
Calm	Credibility	Family	Insightful
Candor	Curiosity	Fame	Inspiration
Capacity	Decisiveness	Fearlessness	Integrity
Caution	Dedication	Focus	Intelligence
Certainty	Dependability	Foresight	Intensity
Challenge	Determination	Fortitude	Intuitive
Charity	Development	Freedom	Joy
Clarity	Devotion	Friendship	Justice
Cleanliness	Dignity	Fun	Kindness
Clever	Diligence	Generosity	Knowledge
Collaboration	Discipline	Genius	Lawfulness
Comfort	Discovery	Goodness	Leadership

Learning Humans

Learning
Liberty
Logic
Love
Loyalty
Mastery
Maturity
Meaning
Moderation
Motivation
Openness
Optimism
Order
Organization
Originality
Passion
Patience
Peace
Performance
Persistence
Playfulness
Poise
Potential
Power
Presentness
Productivity
Professionalism
Prosperity
Purpose
Quality
Realism
Reason
Recognition
Reflection
Relationships

Respect
Responsibility
Restraint
Results-oriented
Reverence
Rigor
Risk
Satisfaction
Security
Self-reliance
Selflessness
Sensitivity
Serenity
Service
Sharing
Significance
Silence
Simplicity
Sincerity
Skillfulness
Solitude
Spirituality
Spontaneity
Stability
Status
Stewardship
Strength
Structure
Success
Support
Surprise
Sustainability
Talent
Teamwork

Temperance
Thoroughness
Thoughtfulness
Timeliness
Tolerance
Toughness
Tranquility
Transparency
Trust
Trustworthiness
Truth
Understanding
Uniqueness
Unity
Valor
Vigor
Vision
Vitality
Wealth
Winning
Wisdom
Wonder

Values you'd like to add:

What TOP 3 values will define your practice this year?

You'll reiterate and remind yourself of these throughout the planner.

1.

2.

3.

Calendaring is a Verb

If you're planning to stay, you'll need to consider all of the calendars that are in and which impact your life.

For this activity, gather them together: paper planners, online calendars, district academic calendars and curriculum maps, etc. You'll also need access to the calendars of important people in your life (or, if not their whole calendar, dates of events that matter to them).

We'll build your calendar to support your values-connected practice by using it to represent all parts of you and your practice. If, at any point, there is some part of your life that is important to you that isn't listed here, please add it - and, more importantly, get it on your calendar!

Use the following checklist to add directly to your planner:

Systemic Structure
Academic Calendar Dates
- [ ] 1st contract day
- [ ] Last contract day
- [ ] 1st day of classes
- [ ] End of term/Start of term
- [ ] Holidays

Educator Obligations
*Keep in mind: Even if you don't know the exact dates of all of these obligations, you know these things will happen. Protecting time on your calendar for them, and knowing that you have accounted for that time which can move around, will prevent them from surprising you - and support proactive scheduling that works best for you:
- [ ] Back to School Night (or similar)
- [ ] Family/Educator conferences (or similar)
- [ ] Dates/times grades are due for each term
- [ ] Faculty/staff meetings
- [ ] PLC/Collaboration meetings
- [ ] Testing windows - benchmarks
- [ ] Testing windows - end-of-levels
- [ ] Committee meetings
- [ ] Coaching/after school programs
- [ ] "Banquets," dances, field days, or other school-related events
- [ ] Administrator observations
- [ ] Administrator evaluations
- [ ] Additional meetings re: next year's course assignments
- [ ] Additional obligations you'd like to add:

Calendaring is a Verb

Your Life
Personal Have-To's
☐ Routine health appointments: now that you know your school obligations, schedule appointments NOW, so that the time is protected, and you all-of-a-sudden go 3 years without getting your teeth cleaned. It's tempting to save this for Summer. Please don't.
    ☐ doctor(s)
    ☐ dentist
    ☐ other specialists:
☐ Financial/legal deadlines (when rent is due, court dates, etc.)
☐ Routine auto maintenance (oil change, pre-vacation inspections, etc)

Personal Want-To's
*Consider doing this step several times, both before the school year starts and after the first term ends, with different people in your life who you'd like to plan with, particularly if they are not educators.
☐ Your birthday (It doesn't matter how you feel about it, no one's forcing you to take the day off. Just get it on the calendar because this calendar is your LIFE, and it's ok to acknowledge the adventure's anniversary. You matter, even if the anniversary of your birth occurs during the school year.)
☐ Family/friend birthdays
☐ Events/festivals/seasonal or time-sensitive opportunities (ex: If you hate hot weather, but love being outside, you might protect some autumn/spring time)

Inspiring Instruction
☐ Final project deadlines: This is NOT the same as the end of the term, NOR the day that grades are due. Consider making final projects, or anything summative that requires time to grade, due well before your grades are due, even if that means it's due a week or two before the actual end of the term.
☐ Grading: When, exactly, will you actually grade the above-mentioned final projects? Is this timeline likely to change? Yes. Are you more likely to stay sane if you represent the actual time it's going to take on your calendar, so that you don't bail on important parts of your life 3-4 times a year because grades are predictably due? Also yes.
☐ High-Stress Periods: Mark times that are more intense for you, personally, as a date range that you may need to lighten up in other areas (ex: plan a familiar unit during this time, or avoid an energy-intensive-but-probably-fun-camping trip requiring lots of last-minute planning)
☐ Low-Morale Periods: Mark times that you tend to struggle with morale (Feb/March are common for teachers)). Intentionally plan units and learning episodes that you're excited about personally during these times.
☐ Catch-Up/Catch-It days: when will you make changes to lessons you've tried in the actual instructions/worksheets/materials, so that it's ready to go next time? When will you tidy grades to account for absences, make-up work, etc? Don't save this to the end of the term/year!

Tracking Your Self-Care Landscape

Make a list of all of the ways you like to spend your time. List activities you engage in daily or weekly. Also include activities that you value and enjoy but engage in less frequently, and activities that might only be dreams this point.

Once you've listed the activities that you enjoy, evaluate if you utilize them for coping (pushing "pause" on feelings/the world and returning to an unchanged world when your coping activity concludes) or caring (being present with how you're feeling and engaging in a way that your world has shifted for the better when you're done).

Stuff I Like To Do	Coping or Caring	Intelectual	Physical.	Social	Emotional	Spiritual

Learning Humans

School-Year Focal Components of Self-Care

Consider the activities you evaluated on the previous page. Which component/s of self-care could use more attention? Use this table to consider how you'll fortify and round-out your self-care approach to intentionally include all categories.

Component	Definition/Examples	How will you care for this part of yourself/your life this school year?
Intellectual	Opportunities to be interested, curious, creative, and take risks in learning. Examples: Book club Garage tinkering Hobbies that require learning	
Physical	Acknowledges that you have a body, and that movement, diet, and exercise play an essential role in your well-being Examples: Shoulder shrugs waiting for the copier 3x30 min HIIT workouts Deep breaths while taking attendance	
Social	Even the most introverted need social interaction adult-to-adult. Examples: Watch party with a friend Quarterly potlucks with neighbors Weekly friend calls while folding laundry	
Emotional	Name your emotions and allow yourself to feel them (ideally without judgement) Examples: Journaling Talking to a trusted friend Attending a support group/therapy	
Spiritual	Connection to something larger/more meaningful than your own life. Examples: Volunteering for a cause you value Attending a faith community service Appreciating nature	

Learning Humans

Protecting Time for Self-Care

Now it's time to map out how your self-care lives in your day-to-day plans. Use this checklist to populate your calendar with your self-care foci.

☐ **Calendar one high-value self-care activity per week**
   High-value self-care activities are those which satisfy two or more categories from your "Stuff I Like to Do" list. For example, rather than running on a treadmill (physical) i might plan a hike with a friend (physical, social, emotional, spiritual)

☐ **Calendar one "look forward to" event each month**
   If there are times without events, birthdays, etc., plan something specific that you'll look forward to, (for example a movie with friends or cooking something new that you've wanted to try.

☐ **Pick 1 hour per weekday when you will NOT be working**
   This may not include your commute, nor when you're trying to sleep.

☐ **Pick one weekend day every weekend when you will NOT be working**
   It's ok if it changes week to week, but can also be helpful to keep consistent. Consider communicating this day to the people in your life with whom you want to stay connected. Letting them know that you're most likely able to keep plans the night before this day and this day itself will help them to honor your boundaries while also getting to hang out with you.

☐ **Use your email signature and policy documents to communicate boundaries**
   Focus on boundaries* which, if you were clear about, would both protect your time and support positive communication expectations for colleagues, students, and families.
   *Note - framing things as positives "I check email once per day, and will respond within 48 working hours" may make your life easier than "My personal time is my personal time, your emergency isn't my emergency, I'll get to your email when I can during contract hours."

Learning Humans

Life Routines for Self-Care

Task	Days/Times	General Places
Grocery shopping/pickup		
Food prep for the week		
Eating		
Breakfast		
Lunch		
Dinner		
Laundry		
Housecleaning		
Selecting clothes for work		
Work email		
Personal email		
Personal phone (appointments, etc)		
Lesson planning		
Evaluating/entering grades		
Drink water during schoolday		
Take 3 deep, slow breaths during schoolday		
Pee during schooldays		
Other physical care during school day:		
Start-of-Day transition ritual		
End-of-Day transition ritual		

Classroom Routines for Mental Spaciousness

Routines help to fight decision fatigue! Free your brain for the decisions that matter by deciding once for as many activities, actions, and choices as possible.

The tasks that keep your life running require time. I can often be tough to protect that time moment-by-moment. Planning can take some of the stress out of every-day decision-making.

In the classroom

Here are some (but not all) of the things you may want to "decide ahead" (cross-checking with school policy, of course):

Tardiness

- ☐ How tardy is tardy? Seats in chairs at the bell or tardy? Make that explicit! Soft start at bell, hard start at 3 mins after? Make that explicit!
- ☐ How will students know a tardy has been recorded?
  What is the incentive, from the students' perspective, to be on time? Note: an incentive needs to be positive; avoiding conflict/shame shouldn't be a goal we encourage for students, they already have to manage enough of that by simply existing.

Absences

- ☐ What assignments/types of assignments can be made-up?
- ☐ What assignments require substitution activities (because they can't be replicated outside of class)?
- ☐ How do you want students to tell you they'll be absent?
- ☐ How do students figure out what work they missed, ideally without needing to ask you nor other students about it (at least to find the thing)?
- ☐ How do students submit make-up work? What is the make-up work deadline?

Bathroom Visits

- ☐ How many visits, per unit time, is a fair and reasonable number for an average student to need?
- ☐ How long do you consider a bathroom break? Who tracks that?
- ☐ What is the reward for students who don't utilize their breaks? This isn't a penalty for those who may have conditions that necessitate breaks, it's a quiet acknowledgement for those who can and do stay in class.

"Take A Breather" procedures

- ☐ How do you support students to resolve interpersonal conflict?
- ☐ How can students step away if/when they're feeling overwhelmed and/or dysregulated?

Learning Humans

Prepare for the Best, Plan for the Worst

Transition rituals support you to be as present as the best version of yourself as possible when going from life to school and back again. And sometimes life follows us into the classroom, so it's good to be prepared.

Transition Ritual: Life to School
How will you mark the transition to teaching in the morning?
Examples:

- take 3 deep breaths as my computer is turning on, and state my values out loud
- Take my ID from the glovebox, and as I put the lanyard around my neck, say an affirmation to myself to honor what I'm bringing to the day.

Transition Ritual: Life to School
How will you mark the transition to back to life at the end of the day?
Examples:

- take 3 deep breaths as I wash my hands/face, visualizing what ideas/feelings I can leave at school to pick up the next day
- Place my ID back in the glovebox, and as I do, say out loud "Today I gave .... to my practice and my students, tonight I'll give .... to myself and the people I care about in my life."

When You Have a Body in the Classroom
Here's a list of things you may want to prepare to support a potentially rough day in the classroom to be less rough (this is not medical advice, ask your doctor for confirmation):

Over-the-counter:
- [ ] Ibuprofen/NSAID
- [ ] Antacids
- [ ] Anti-diarrhea
- [ ] Anti-histamines
- [ ] Cough drops
- [ ] Cold/Flu medicine

- [ ] A change of clothes
- [ ] Non-perishable snacks
- [ ] Non-perishable emergency lunch options
- [ ] A bowl, plate, and cutlery
- [ ] Extra water bottles
- [ ] Safety pins/Small sewing kit

Learning Humans

Instruction-Imbedded Self-Care: Supporting Your Students

Component	Examples	What might you try?
Intellectual	▪ Gather student questions to inform next instructional steps ▪ Build a "wonder Wall" where students can post ideas that inspire awe	
Physical	▪ Plan opportunities for students to get up to cross the room (for materials/ handouts) at strategic times to intentionally break up instruction ▪ Build in opportunities to move in impromptu ways (ex: big arm point to a resource on a wall)	
Social	▪ Offer students questions to interact with each other at transitions ▪ Line up students to support each other based on different skills, being explicit about the strengths both bring to an interaction	
Emotional	▪ Use written prompts to support students to name any feelings they're having. This can be utilized about class content, assignments, or about out-of-class experiences.	
Spiritual	▪ Plan opportunities for students to get up to cross the room (for materials/ handouts) at strategic times to intentionally break up instruction	

Learning Humans

Instruction-Imbedded Self-Care Template

Please feel free to use this template by either photocopying (this text counts as permission to copy with attribution), or by re-creating in a digital format for increased flexibility and repeatability.

Lesson Title	
Standard/s	

Which value/s motivate this lesson, and how are they explicitly supported?

Learning Objective (by the end of the lesson, students will be able to...)	To demonstrate learning, students will: Students will know if they learned/ understood by:

	In order to support a learning community,	Care for Self and Students (mark A (adult) when the lesson meets your needs, and S when an activity supports students, in whichever column applies)				
Time	Students Will	I will	Intelectual	Physical	Social	Emotional	Spiritual

Based on how today went, tomorrow I want to make sure to:

How Will You Know Your Planning Is Working?

Guiding Values	1. 2. 3.
Realm	If you are successful at "planning to stay," what will you know, feel, and be able to do?
Classroom: My INTERNAL Experience	I will know: I will feel: I will be able to:
Classroom: My EXTERNAL Experience	I will know: I will feel: I will be able to:
Personal Life: My INTERNAL Experience	I will know: I will feel: I will be able to:
Personal Life: My EXTERNAL Experience	I will know: I will feel: Be Able to Do:

How Will You Know Your Planning Is Working?

Guiding Values	1. 2. 3.
Realm	If you are successful at "planning to stay," what will you know, feel, and be able to do?
Classroom: My INTERNAL Experience	I will know: I will feel: I will be able to:
Classroom: My EXTERNAL Experience	I will know: I will feel: I will be able to:
Personal Life: My INTERNAL Experience	I will know: I will feel: I will be able to:
Personal Life: My EXTERNAL Experience	I will know: I will feel: Be Able to Do:

Learning Humans

How Will You Know Your Planning Is Working?

Guiding Values	1. 2. 3.
Realm	If you are successful at "planning to stay," what will you know, feel, and be able to do?
Classroom: My INTERNAL Experience	I will know: I will feel: I will be able to:
Classroom: My EXTERNAL Experience	I will know: I will feel: I will be able to:
Personal Life: My INTERNAL Experience	I will know: I will feel: I will be able to:
Personal Life: My EXTERNAL Experience	I will know: I will feel: Be Able to Do:

How Will You Know Your Planning Is Working?

Guiding Values	1. 2. 3.
Realm	If you are successful at "planning to stay," what will you know, feel, and be able to do?
Classroom: My INTERNAL Experience	I will know: I will feel: I will be able to:
Classroom: My EXTERNAL Experience	I will know: I will feel: I will be able to:
Personal Life: My INTERNAL Experience	I will know: I will feel: I will be able to:
Personal Life: My EXTERNAL Experience	I will know: I will feel: Be Able to Do:

Learning Humans

How Will You Know Your Planning Is Working?

Guiding Values	1. 2. 3.
Realm	If you are successful at "planning to stay," what will you know, feel, and be able to do?
Classroom: My INTERNAL Experience	I will know: I will feel: I will be able to:
Classroom: My EXTERNAL Experience	I will know: I will feel: I will be able to:
Personal Life: My INTERNAL Experience	I will know: I will feel: I will be able to:
Personal Life: My EXTERNAL Experience	I will know: I will feel: Be Able to Do:

How Will You Know Your Planning Is Working?

Guiding Values	1. 2. 3.
Realm	If you are successful at "planning to stay," what will you know, feel, and be able to do?
Classroom: My INTERNAL Experience	I will know: I will feel: I will be able to:
Classroom: My EXTERNAL Experience	I will know: I will feel: I will be able to:
Personal Life: My INTERNAL Experience	I will know: I will feel: I will be able to:
Personal Life: My EXTERNAL Experience	I will know: I will feel: Be Able to Do:

Learning Humans

How Will You Know Your Planning Is Working?

Guiding Values	1. 2. 3.
Realm	If you are successful at "planning to stay," what will you know, feel, and be able to do?
Classroom: My INTERNAL Experience	I will know: I will feel: I will be able to:
Classroom: My EXTERNAL Experience	I will know: I will feel: I will be able to:
Personal Life: My INTERNAL Experience	I will know: I will feel: I will be able to:
Personal Life: My EXTERNAL Experience	I will know: I will feel: Be Able to Do:

How Will You Know Your Planning Is Working?

Guiding Values	1. 2. 3.
Realm	If you are successful at "planning to stay," what will you know, feel, and be able to do?
Classroom: My INTERNAL Experience	I will know: I will feel: I will be able to:
Classroom: My EXTERNAL Experience	I will know: I will feel: I will be able to:
Personal Life: My INTERNAL Experience	I will know: I will feel: I will be able to:
Personal Life: My EXTERNAL Experience	I will know: I will feel: Be Able to Do:

Learning Humans

How Will You Know Your Planning Is Working?

Guiding Values	1. 2. 3.
Realm	If you are successful at "planning to stay," what will you know, feel, and be able to do?
Classroom: My INTERNAL Experience	I will know: I will feel: I will be able to:
Classroom: My EXTERNAL Experience	I will know: I will feel: I will be able to:
Personal Life: My INTERNAL Experience	I will know: I will feel: I will be able to:
Personal Life: My EXTERNAL Experience	I will know: I will feel: Be Able to Do:

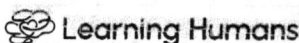

Monthly Calendar

Month:

Planning to Stay	Monday	Tuesday	Wednesday
Self-care priorities (list specific activities): ⬤ Intellectual:			
⬤ Physical:			
⬤ Social:			
⬤ Emotional:			
⬤ Spiritual:			
Track your progress: every day that you meet a self-care need, check the component, like this: ✓ ✓			
*be sure to calendar one event this month that you're really excited about!			

Guiding Values:

Thursday	Friday	Saturday	Sunday

Month:

Planning to Stay	Monday	Tuesday	Wednesday
Self-care priorities (list specific activities): Intellectual:	☐	☐	☐
Physical:	☐	☐	☐
Social:			
Emotional:	☐	☐	☐
Spiritual:			
Track your progress: every day that you meet a self-care need, check the component, like this: ✓ ✓ *be sure to calendar one event this month that you're really excited about!	☐	☐	☐
	☐	☐	☐

Learning Humans

Guiding Values:

Thursday	Friday	Saturday	Sunday

Month:

Planning to Stay	Monday	Tuesday	Wednesday
Self-care priorities (list specific activities): Intellectual:			
Physical:			
Social:			
Emotional:			
Spiritual:			
Track your progress: every day that you meet a self-care need, check the component, like this: *be sure to calendar one event this month that you're really excited about!			

Learning Humans

Guiding Values:

Thursday	Friday	Saturday	Sunday

Month:

Planning to Stay	Monday	Tuesday	Wednesday
Self-care priorities (list specific activities):	☐	☐	☐
Intellectual:			
Physical:	☐	☐	☐
Social:			
Emotional:	☐	☐	☐
Spiritual:			
Track your progress: every day that you meet a self-care need, check the component, like this:	☐	☐	☐
✓ ✓			
*be sure to calendar one event this month that you're really excited about!	☐	☐	☐

Guiding Values:

Thursday	Friday	Saturday	Sunday

Month:

Planning to Stay	Monday	Tuesday	Wednesday
Self-care priorities (list specific activities):	☐	☐	☐
Intellectual:			
Physical:	☐	☐	☐
Social:			
Emotional:	☐	☐	☐
Spiritual:			
Track your progress: every day that you meet a self-care need, check the component, like this:	☐	☐	☐
*be sure to calendar one event this month that you're really excited about!	☐	☐	☐

Learning Humans

Guiding Values:

Thursday	Friday	Saturday	Sunday

Month:

Planning to Stay	Monday	Tuesday	Wednesday
Self-care priorities (list specific activities): Intellectual: Physical: Social: Emotional: Spiritual: **Track your progress:** every day that you meet a self-care need, check the component, like this: ✓ ✓ *be sure to calendar one event this month that you're really excited about!			

Guiding Values:

Thursday	Friday	Saturday	Sunday

Month:

Planning to Stay	Monday	Tuesday	Wednesday
Self-care priorities (list specific activities):	☐	☐	☐
Intellectual:			
Physical:	☐	☐	☐
Social:			
Emotional:	☐	☐	☐
Spiritual:			
Track your progress: every day that you meet a self-care need, check the component, like this:	☐	☐	☐
*be sure to calendar one event this month that you're really excited about!	☐	☐	☐

Learning Humans

Guiding Values:

Thursday	Friday	Saturday	Sunday

Month:

Planning to Stay	Monday	Tuesday	Wednesday
Self-care priorities (list specific activities): ⭐ Intellectual:	☐	☐	☐
🧍 Physical:	☐	☐	☐
🫂 Social:			
❤️ Emotional:	☐	☐	☐
🌸 Spiritual:			
Track your progress: every day that you meet a self-care need, check the component, like this: ⭐ ✓ 🧍 ❤️ ✓ *be sure to calendar one event this month that you're really excited about!	☐	☐	☐
	☐	☐	☐

Learning Humans

Guiding Values:

Thursday	Friday	Saturday	Sunday

Month:

Planning to Stay	Monday	Tuesday	Wednesday
Self-care priorities (list specific activities): Intellectual:	☐	☐	☐
Physical:	☐	☐	☐
Social:	☐	☐	☐
Emotional:	☐	☐	☐
Spiritual:	☐	☐	☐
Track your progress: every day that you meet a self-care need, check the component, like this: ✓ ✓ *be sure to calendar one event this month that you're really excited about!	☐	☐	☐

Learning Humans

Guiding Values:

Thursday	Friday	Saturday	Sunday
☐	☐	☐	☐
☐	☐	☐	☐
☐	☐	☐	☐
☐	☐	☐	☐
☐	☐	☐	☐

Month:

Planning to Stay	Monday	Tuesday	Wednesday
Self-care priorities (list specific activities): Intellectual:	☐	☐	☐
Physical:	☐	☐	☐
Social:			
Emotional:	☐	☐	☐
Spiritual:			
Track your progress: every day that you meet a self-care need, check the component, like this: *be sure to calendar one event this month that you're really excited about!	☐	☐	☐
	☐	☐	☐

Learning Humans

Guiding Values:

Thursday	Friday	Saturday	Sunday

Month:

Planning to Stay	Monday	Tuesday	Wednesday
Self-care priorities (list specific activities):	☐	☐	☐
Intellectual:			
Physical:	☐	☐	☐
Social:			
Emotional:	☐	☐	☐
Spiritual:			
	☐	☐	☐
Track your progress: every day that you meet a self-care need, check the component, like this:			
	☐	☐	☐
*be sure to calendar one event this month that you're really excited about!			

Learning Humans

Guiding Values:

Thursday	Friday	Saturday	Sunday

Month:

Planning to Stay	Monday	Tuesday	Wednesday
Self-care priorities (list specific activities):	☐	☐	☐
Intellectual:			
Physical:	☐	☐	☐
Social:			
Emotional:	☐	☐	☐
Spiritual:			
Track your progress: every day that you meet a self-care need, check the component, like this:	☐	☐	☐
*be sure to calendar one event this month that you're really excited about!	☐	☐	☐

Guiding Values:

Thursday	Friday	Saturday	Sunday
☐	☐	☐	☐
☐	☐	☐	☐
☐	☐	☐	☐
☐	☐	☐	☐
☐	☐	☐	☐

Weekly Calendar

Time	Monday /	Tuesday /	Wednesday /	Guiding Values:
6am				
7am				
8am				
9am				Interwoven with your general curriculum plans calendar specific times for these activities (selecting times that will minimize your stress):
10am				
11am				**Own Your Time**
12pm				▪ 1 high-value self-care activity/week
1pm				▪ 1 work-free hour/day ▪ Which weekend day will be work-free? Circle: Saturday Sunday
2pm				
3pm				**Own Your Classroom:**
4pm				▪ Lesson planning (keep this time-bound, or it will take all you give it!)
5pm				▪ Evaluating (anything students can't self/ peer grade)
6pm				▪ Entering grades ▪ Making copies ▪ Gathering materials
7pm				▪ Other admin tasks (responding to email, positive calls home, etc)
8pm				
	Today I gave my practice: Tonight I'll give my life:	Today I gave my practice: Tonight I'll give my life:	Today I gave my practice: Tonight I'll give my life:	

Learning Humans

Time	Thursday /	Friday /	Saturday /	Sunday /
6am				
7am				
8am				
9am				
10am				
11am				
12pm				
1pm				
2pm				
3pm				
4pm				
5pm				
6pm				
7pm				
8pm				
	Today I gave my practice: Tonight I'll give my life:	Today I gave my practice: Tonight I'll give my life:	Today I gave my practice: Tonight I'll give my life:	Today I gave my practice: Tonight I'll give my life:

Learning Humans

Time	Monday /	Tuesday /	Wednesday /	Guiding Values:
6am				
7am				
8am				
9am				Interwoven with your general curriculum plans calendar specific times for these activities (selecting times that will minimize your stress):
10am				
11am				
12pm				**Own Your Time**
1pm				• 1 high-value self-care activity/week • 1 work-free hour/day • Which weekend day will be work-free? Circle:
2pm				Saturday Sunday
3pm				**Own Your Classroom:**
4pm				• Lesson planning (keep this time-bound, or it will take all you give it!)
5pm				• Evaluating (anything students can't self/peer grade)
6pm				• Entering grades • Making copies • Gathering materials
7pm				• Other admin tasks (responding to email, positive calls home, etc)
8pm				
	Today I gave my practice: Tonight I'll give my life:	Today I gave my practice: Tonight I'll give my life:	Today I gave my practice: Tonight I'll give my life:	

Learning Humans

Time	Thursday /	Friday /	Saturday /	Sunday /
6am				
7am				
8am				
9am				
10am				
11am				
12pm				
1pm				
2pm				
3pm				
4pm				
5pm				
6pm				
7pm				
8pm				
	Today I gave my practice: Tonight I'll give my life:	Today I gave my practice: Tonight I'll give my life:	Today I gave my practice: Tonight I'll give my life:	Today I gave my practice: Tonight I'll give my life:

Learning Humans

Time	Monday /	Tuesday /	Wednesday /	Guiding Values:
6am				
7am				
8am				
9am				Interwoven with your general curriculum plans calendar specific times for these activities (selecting times that will minimize your stress):
10am				
11am				**Own Your Time** • 1 high-value self-care activity/week
12pm				• 1 work-free hour/day
1pm				• Which weekend day will be work-free? Circle:
2pm				Saturday Sunday
3pm				**Own Your Classroom:** • Lesson planning (keep this time-bound, or it will take all you give it!)
4pm				• Evaluating (anything students can't self/peer grade)
5pm				• Entering grades
6pm				• Making copies • Gathering materials
7pm				• Other admin tasks (responding to email, positive calls home, etc)
8pm				
	Today I gave my practice: Tonight I'll give my life:	Today I gave my practice: Tonight I'll give my life:	Today I gave my practice: Tonight I'll give my life:	

Learning Humans

Time	Thursday /	Friday /	Saturday /	Sunday /
6am				
7am				
8am				
9am				
10am				
11am				
12pm				
1pm				
2pm				
3pm				
4pm				
5pm				
6pm				
7pm				
8pm				
	Today I gave my practice:	Today I gave my practice:	Today I gave my practice:	Today I gave my practice:
	Tonight I'll give my life:	Tonight I'll give my life:	Tonight I'll give my life:	Tonight I'll give my life:

Learning Humans

Time	Monday /	Tuesday /	Wednesday /	Guiding Values:
6am				
7am				
8am				
9am				Interwoven with your general curriculum plans calendar specific times for these activities (selecting times that will minimize your stress):
10am				
11am				
12pm				
1pm				
2pm				
3pm				
4pm				
5pm				
6pm				
7pm				
8pm				

Own Your Time
- 1 high-value self-care activity/week
- 1 work-free hour/day
- Which weekend day will be work-free?
  Circle:

  Saturday Sunday

Own Your Classroom:
- Lesson planning (keep this time-bound, or it will take all you give it!)
- Evaluating (anything students can't self/peer grade)
- Entering grades
- Making copies
- Gathering materials
- Other admin tasks (responding to email, positive calls home, etc)

Monday	Tuesday	Wednesday
Today I gave my practice:	Today I gave my practice:	Today I gave my practice:
Tonight I'll give my life:	Tonight I'll give my life:	Tonight I'll give my life:

Learning Humans

Time	Thursday /	Friday /	Saturday /	Sunday /
6am				
7am				
8am				
9am				
10am				
11am				
12pm				
1pm				
2pm				
3pm				
4pm				
5pm				
6pm				
7pm				
8pm				
	Today I gave my practice: Tonight I'll give my life:	Today I gave my practice: Tonight I'll give my life:	Today I gave my practice: Tonight I'll give my life:	Today I gave my practice: Tonight I'll give my life:

Learning Humans

Time	Monday /	Tuesday /	Wednesday /	Guiding Values:
6am				
7am				
8am				
9am				Interwoven with your general curriculum plans calendar specific times for these activities (selecting times that will minimize your stress):
10am				
11am				**Own Your Time**
12pm				- 1 high-value self-care activity/week
1pm				- 1 work-free hour/day
2pm				- Which weekend day will be work-free? Circle: Saturday Sunday
3pm				**Own Your Classroom:**
4pm				- Lesson planning (keep this time-bound, or it will take all you give it!)
5pm				- Evaluating (anything students can't self/peer grade)
6pm				- Entering grades
7pm				- Making copies
				- Gathering materials
8pm				- Other admin tasks (responding to email, positive calls home, etc)
	Today I gave my practice: Tonight I'll give my life:	Today I gave my practice: Tonight I'll give my life:	Today I gave my practice: Tonight I'll give my life:	

Learning Humans

Time	Thursday /	Friday /	Saturday /	Sunday /
6am				
7am				
8am				
9am				
10am				
11am				
12pm				
1pm				
2pm				
3pm				
4pm				
5pm				
6pm				
7pm				
8pm				
	Today I gave my practice: Tonight I'll give my life:	Today I gave my practice: Tonight I'll give my life:	Today I gave my practice: Tonight I'll give my life:	Today I gave my practice: Tonight I'll give my life:

Time	Monday /	Tuesday /	Wednesday /	Guiding Values:
6am				
7am				
8am				
9am				Interwoven with your general curriculum plans calendar specific times for these activities (selecting times that will minimize your stress):
10am				
11am				
12pm				**Own Your Time**
1pm				
2pm				
3pm				**Own Your Classroom:**
4pm				
5pm				
6pm				
7pm				
8pm				

Own Your Time
- 1 high-value self-care activity/week
- 1 work-free hour/day
- Which weekend day will be work-free? Circle:

  Saturday Sunday

Own Your Classroom:
- Lesson planning (keep this time-bound, or it will take all you give it!)
- Evaluating (anything students can't self/peer grade)
- Entering grades
- Making copies
- Gathering materials
- Other admin tasks (responding to email, positive calls home, etc)

Today I gave my practice:	Today I gave my practice:	Today I gave my practice:
Tonight I'll give my life:	Tonight I'll give my life:	Tonight I'll give my life:

Learning Humans

Time	Thursday /	Friday /	Saturday /	Sunday /
6am				
7am				
8am				
9am				
10am				
11am				
12pm				
1pm				
2pm				
3pm				
4pm				
5pm				
6pm				
7pm				
8pm				
	Today I gave my practice: Tonight I'll give my life:	Today I gave my practice: Tonight I'll give my life:	Today I gave my practice: Tonight I'll give my life:	Today I gave my practice: Tonight I'll give my life:

Learning Humans

Time	Monday /	Tuesday /	Wednesday /	Guiding Values:
6am				
7am				
8am				
9am				Interwoven with your general curriculum plans calendar specific times for these activities (selecting times that will minimize your stress):
10am				
11am				**Own Your Time**
12pm				■ 1 high-value self-care activity/week
1pm				■ 1 work-free hour/day ■ Which weekend day will be work-free? Circle:
2pm				Saturday Sunday
3pm				**Own Your Classroom:** ■ Lesson planning (keep this time-bound, or it will take all you give it!)
4pm				
5pm				■ Evaluating (anything students can't self/peer grade)
6pm				■ Entering grades ■ Making copies ■ Gathering materials
7pm				■ Other admin tasks (responding to email, positive calls home, etc)
8pm				
	Today I gave my practice:

Tonight I'll give my life: | Today I gave my practice:

Tonight I'll give my life: | Today I gave my practice:

Tonight I'll give my life: | |

Learning Humans

Time	Thursday /	Friday /	Saturday /	Sunday /
6am				
7am				
8am				
9am				
10am				
11am				
12pm				
1pm				
2pm				
3pm				
4pm				
5pm				
6pm				
7pm				
8pm				
	Today I gave my practice: Tonight I'll give my life:	Today I gave my practice: Tonight I'll give my life:	Today I gave my practice: Tonight I'll give my life:	Today I gave my practice: Tonight I'll give my life:

Learning Humans

Time	Monday /	Tuesday /	Wednesday /	Guiding Values:
6am				
7am				
8am				
9am				Interwoven with your general curriculum plans calendar specific times for these activities (selecting times that will minimize your stress):
10am				
11am				**Own Your Time**
12pm				• 1 high-value self-care activity/week
1pm				• 1 work-free hour/day
2pm				• Which weekend day will be work-free? Circle: Saturday Sunday
3pm				**Own Your Classroom:**
4pm				• Lesson planning (keep this time-bound, or it will take all you give it!)
5pm				• Evaluating (anything students can't self/peer grade)
6pm				• Entering grades
7pm				• Making copies • Gathering materials
8pm				• Other admin tasks (responding to email, positive calls home, etc)
	Today I gave my practice: Tonight I'll give my life:	Today I gave my practice: Tonight I'll give my life:	Today I gave my practice: Tonight I'll give my life:	

Learning Humans

Time	Thursday /	Friday /	Saturday /	Sunday /
6am				
7am				
8am				
9am				
10am				
11am				
12pm				
1pm				
2pm				
3pm				
4pm				
5pm				
6pm				
7pm				
8pm				
	Today I gave my practice: Tonight I'll give my life:	Today I gave my practice: Tonight I'll give my life:	Today I gave my practice: Tonight I'll give my life:	Today I gave my practice: Tonight I'll give my life:

Time	Monday /	Tuesday /	Wednesday /	**Guiding Values:**
6am				
7am				
8am				
9am				Interwoven with your general curriculum plans calendar specific times for these activities (selecting times that will minimize your stress):
10am				
11am				**Own Your Time**
12pm				▪ 1 high-value self-care activity/week
1pm				▪ 1 work-free hour/day ▪ Which weekend day will be work-free? Circle: Saturday Sunday
2pm				
3pm				**Own Your Classroom:** ▪ Lesson planning (keep this time-bound, or it will take all you give it!)
4pm				
5pm				▪ Evaluating (anything students can't self/peer grade)
6pm				▪ Entering grades ▪ Making copies
7pm				▪ Gathering materials ▪ Other admin tasks (responding to email, positive calls home, etc)
8pm				
	Today I gave my practice: Tonight I'll give my life:	Today I gave my practice: Tonight I'll give my life:	Today I gave my practice: Tonight I'll give my life:	

Learning Humans

Time	Thursday /	Friday /	Saturday /	Sunday /
6am				
7am				
8am				
9am				
10am				
11am				
12pm				
1pm				
2pm				
3pm				
4pm				
5pm				
6pm				
7pm				
8pm				
	Today I gave my practice: Tonight I'll give my life:	Today I gave my practice: Tonight I'll give my life:	Today I gave my practice: Tonight I'll give my life:	Today I gave my practice: Tonight I'll give my life:

Time	Monday /	Tuesday /	Wednesday /	Guiding Values:
6am				
7am				
8am				
9am				Interwoven with your general curriculum plans calendar specific times for these activities (selecting times that will minimize your stress):
10am				
11am				**Own Your Time**
12pm				■ 1 high-value self-care activity/week
1pm				■ 1 work-free hour/day ■ Which weekend day will be work-free? Circle:
2pm				Saturday Sunday
3pm				**Own Your Classroom:** ■ Lesson planning (keep this time-bound, or it will take all you give it!)
4pm				
5pm				■ Evaluating (anything students can't self/peer grade)
6pm				■ Entering grades ■ Making copies
7pm				■ Gathering materials ■ Other admin tasks (responding to email, positive calls home, etc)
8pm				
	Today I gave my practice: Tonight I'll give my life:	Today I gave my practice: Tonight I'll give my life:	Today I gave my practice: Tonight I'll give my life:	

Learning Humans

Time	Thursday /	Friday /	Saturday /	Sunday /
6am				
7am				
8am				
9am				
10am				
11am				
12pm				
1pm				
2pm				
3pm				
4pm				
5pm				
6pm				
7pm				
8pm				
	Today I gave my practice: Tonight I'll give my life:	Today I gave my practice: Tonight I'll give my life:	Today I gave my practice: Tonight I'll give my life:	Today I gave my practice: Tonight I'll give my life:

Time	Monday /	Tuesday /	Wednesday /	Guiding Values:
6am				
7am				
8am				
9am				
10am				Interwoven with your general curriculum plans calendar specific times for these activities (selecting times that will minimize your stress):
11am				
12pm				
1pm				
2pm				
3pm				
4pm				
5pm				
6pm				
7pm				
8pm				

Own Your Time
- 1 high-value self-care activity/week
- 1 work-free hour/day
- Which weekend day will be work-free?
  Circle:

  Saturday Sunday

Own Your Classroom:
- Lesson planning (keep this time-bound, or it will take all you give it!)
- Evaluating (anything students can't self/peer grade)
- Entering grades
- Making copies
- Gathering materials
- Other admin tasks (responding to email, positive calls home, etc)

Monday	Tuesday	Wednesday
Today I gave my practice:	Today I gave my practice:	Today I gave my practice:
Tonight I'll give my life:	Tonight I'll give my life:	Tonight I'll give my life:

Learning Humans

Time	Thursday /	Friday /	Saturday /	Sunday /
6am				
7am				
8am				
9am				
10am				
11am				
12pm				
1pm				
2pm				
3pm				
4pm				
5pm				
6pm				
7pm				
8pm				
	Today I gave my practice: Tonight I'll give my life:	Today I gave my practice: Tonight I'll give my life:	Today I gave my practice: Tonight I'll give my life:	Today I gave my practice: Tonight I'll give my life:

Learning Humans

Time	Monday /	Tuesday /	Wednesday /	Guiding Values:
6am				
7am				
8am				
9am				Interwoven with your general curriculum plans calendar specific times for these activities (selecting times that will minimize your stress):
10am				
11am				**Own Your Time**
12pm				▪ 1 high-value self-care activity/week
1pm				▪ 1 work-free hour/day
2pm				▪ Which weekend day will be work-free? Circle: Saturday Sunday
3pm				**Own Your Classroom:**
4pm				▪ Lesson planning (keep this time-bound, or it will take all you give it!)
5pm				▪ Evaluating (anything students can't self/peer grade)
6pm				▪ Entering grades ▪ Making copies
7pm				▪ Gathering materials
8pm				▪ Other admin tasks (responding to email, positive calls home, etc)
	Today I gave my practice: Tonight I'll give my life:	Today I gave my practice: Tonight I'll give my life:	Today I gave my practice: Tonight I'll give my life:	

Learning Humans

Time	Thursday /	Friday /	Saturday /	Sunday /
6am				
7am				
8am				
9am				
10am				
11am				
12pm				
1pm				
2pm				
3pm				
4pm				
5pm				
6pm				
7pm				
8pm				
	Today I gave my practice: Tonight I'll give my life:	Today I gave my practice: Tonight I'll give my life:	Today I gave my practice: Tonight I'll give my life:	Today I gave my practice: Tonight I'll give my life:

Learning Humans

Time	Monday /	Tuesday /	Wednesday /	Guiding Values:
6am				
7am				
8am				
9am				Interwoven with your general curriculum plans calendar specific times for these activities (selecting times that will minimize your stress):
10am				
11am				**Own Your Time**
12pm				■ 1 high-value self-care activity/week
1pm				■ 1 work-free hour/day
2pm				■ Which weekend day will be work-free? Circle: Saturday Sunday
3pm				**Own Your Classroom:**
4pm				■ Lesson planning (keep this time-bound, or it will take all you give it!)
5pm				■ Evaluating (anything students can't self/peer grade)
6pm				■ Entering grades
7pm				■ Making copies
				■ Gathering materials
8pm				■ Other admin tasks (responding to email, positive calls home, etc)
	Today I gave my practice: Tonight I'll give my life:	Today I gave my practice: Tonight I'll give my life:	Today I gave my practice: Tonight I'll give my life:	

Learning Humans

Time	Thursday /	Friday /	Saturday /	Sunday /
6am				
7am				
8am				
9am				
10am				
11am				
12pm				
1pm				
2pm				
3pm				
4pm				
5pm				
6pm				
7pm				
8pm				
	Today I gave my practice: Tonight I'll give my life:	Today I gave my practice: Tonight I'll give my life:	Today I gave my practice: Tonight I'll give my life:	Today I gave my practice: Tonight I'll give my life:

Time	Monday /	Tuesday /	Wednesday /	Guiding Values:
6am				
7am				
8am				
9am				Interwoven with your general curriculum plans calendar specific times for these activities (selecting times that will minimize your stress):
10am				
11am				**Own Your Time**
12pm				▪ 1 high-value self-care activity/week
1pm				▪ 1 work-free hour/day
2pm				▪ Which weekend day will be work-free? Circle: Saturday Sunday
3pm				**Own Your Classroom:**
4pm				▪ Lesson planning (keep this time-bound, or it will take all you give it!)
5pm				▪ Evaluating (anything students can't self/peer grade)
6pm				▪ Entering grades
7pm				▪ Making copies ▪ Gathering materials
8pm				▪ Other admin tasks (responding to email, positive calls home, etc)
	Today I gave my practice:	Today I gave my practice:	Today I gave my practice:	
	Tonight I'll give my life:	Tonight I'll give my life:	Tonight I'll give my life:	

Learning Humans

Time	Thursday /	Friday /	Saturday /	Sunday /
6am				
7am				
8am				
9am				
10am				
11am				
12pm				
1pm				
2pm				
3pm				
4pm				
5pm				
6pm				
7pm				
8pm				
	Today I gave my practice:	Today I gave my practice:	Today I gave my practice:	Today I gave my practice:
	Tonight I'll give my life:	Tonight I'll give my life:	Tonight I'll give my life:	Tonight I'll give my life:

Time	Monday /	Tuesday /	Wednesday /	Guiding Values:
6am				
7am				
8am				
9am				Interwoven with your general curriculum plans calendar specific times for these activities (selecting times that will minimize your stress):
10am				
11am				**Own Your Time**
12pm				▪ 1 high-value self-care activity/week
1pm				▪ 1 work-free hour/day
				▪ Which weekend day will be work-free? Circle:
2pm				Saturday Sunday
3pm				**Own Your Classroom:**
4pm				▪ Lesson planning (keep this time-bound, or it will take all you give it!)
5pm				▪ Evaluating (anything students can't self/peer grade)
6pm				▪ Entering grades
				▪ Making copies
				▪ Gathering materials
7pm				▪ Other admin tasks (responding to email, positive calls home, etc)
8pm				
	Today I gave my practice: Tonight I'll give my life:	Today I gave my practice: Tonight I'll give my life:	Today I gave my practice: Tonight I'll give my life:	

Learning Humans

Time	Thursday /	Friday /	Saturday /	Sunday /
6am				
7am				
8am				
9am				
10am				
11am				
12pm				
1pm				
2pm				
3pm				
4pm				
5pm				
6pm				
7pm				
8pm				
	Today I gave my practice: Tonight I'll give my life:	Today I gave my practice: Tonight I'll give my life:	Today I gave my practice: Tonight I'll give my life:	Today I gave my practice: Tonight I'll give my life:

Time	Monday /	Tuesday /	Wednesday /	Guiding Values:
6am				
7am				
8am				
9am				Interwoven with your general curriculum plans calendar specific times for these activities (selecting times that will minimize your stress):
10am				
11am				**Own Your Time**
12pm				• 1 high-value self-care activity/week
1pm				• 1 work-free hour/day • Which weekend day will be work-free? Circle:
2pm				Saturday Sunday
3pm				**Own Your Classroom:** • Lesson planning (keep this time-bound, or it will take all you give it!)
4pm				
5pm				• Evaluating (anything students can't self/peer grade)
6pm				• Entering grades • Making copies
7pm				• Gathering materials
8pm				• Other admin tasks (responding to email, positive calls home, etc)
	Today I gave my practice: Tonight I'll give my life:	Today I gave my practice: Tonight I'll give my life:	Today I gave my practice: Tonight I'll give my life:	

Learning Humans

Time	Thursday /	Friday /	Saturday /	Sunday /
6am				
7am				
8am				
9am				
10am				
11am				
12pm				
1pm				
2pm				
3pm				
4pm				
5pm				
6pm				
7pm				
8pm				
	Today I gave my practice: Tonight I'll give my life:	Today I gave my practice: Tonight I'll give my life:	Today I gave my practice: Tonight I'll give my life:	Today I gave my practice: Tonight I'll give my life:

Time	Monday /	Tuesday /	Wednesday /	Guiding Values:
6am				
7am				
8am				
9am				Interwoven with your general curriculum plans calendar specific times for these activities (selecting times that will minimize your stress):
10am				
11am				**Own Your Time**
12pm				▪ 1 high-value self-care activity/week
1pm				▪ 1 work-free hour/day ▪ Which weekend day will be work-free? Circle:
2pm				Saturday Sunday
3pm				**Own Your Classroom:** ▪ Lesson planning (keep this time-bound, or it will take all you give it!)
4pm				
5pm				▪ Evaluating (anything students can't self/peer grade)
6pm				▪ Entering grades ▪ Making copies
7pm				▪ Gathering materials ▪ Other admin tasks (responding to email, positive calls home, etc)
8pm				
	Today I gave my practice: Tonight I'll give my life:	Today I gave my practice: Tonight I'll give my life:	Today I gave my practice: Tonight I'll give my life:	

Learning Humans

Time	Thursday /	Friday /	Saturday /	Sunday /
6am				
7am				
8am				
9am				
10am				
11am				
12pm				
1pm				
2pm				
3pm				
4pm				
5pm				
6pm				
7pm				
8pm				
	Today I gave my practice: Tonight I'll give my life:	Today I gave my practice: Tonight I'll give my life:	Today I gave my practice: Tonight I'll give my life:	Today I gave my practice: Tonight I'll give my life:

Learning Humans

Time	Monday /	Tuesday /	Wednesday /	Guiding Values:
6am				
7am				
8am				
9am				Interwoven with your general curriculum plans calendar specific times for these activities (selecting times that will minimize your stress):
10am				
11am				
12pm				**Own Your Time**
1pm				• 1 high-value self-care activity/week
2pm				• 1 work-free hour/day • Which weekend day will be work-free? Circle: Saturday Sunday
3pm				**Own Your Classroom:**
4pm				• Lesson planning (keep this time-bound, or it will take all you give it!)
5pm				• Evaluating (anything students can't self/peer grade)
6pm				• Entering grades • Making copies
7pm				• Gathering materials • Other admin tasks (responding to email, positive calls home, etc)
8pm				
	Today I gave my practice: Tonight I'll give my life:	Today I gave my practice: Tonight I'll give my life:	Today I gave my practice: Tonight I'll give my life:	

Learning Humans

Time	Thursday /	Friday /	Saturday /	Sunday /
6am				
7am				
8am				
9am				
10am				
11am				
12pm				
1pm				
2pm				
3pm				
4pm				
5pm				
6pm				
7pm				
8pm				
	Today I gave my practice:	Today I gave my practice:	Today I gave my practice:	Today I gave my practice:
	Tonight I'll give my life:	Tonight I'll give my life:	Tonight I'll give my life:	Tonight I'll give my life:

Learning Humans

Time	Monday /	Tuesday /	Wednesday /	Guiding Values:
6am				
7am				
8am				
9am				Interwoven with your general curriculum plans calendar specific times for these activities (selecting times that will minimize your stress):
10am				
11am				**Own Your Time**
12pm				▪ 1 high-value self-care activity/week
1pm				▪ 1 work-free hour/day
2pm				▪ Which weekend day will be work-free? Circle:
3pm				Saturday Sunday
4pm				**Own Your Classroom:**
5pm				▪ Lesson planning (keep this time-bound, or it will take all you give it!)
6pm				▪ Evaluating (anything students can't self/peer grade)
7pm				▪ Entering grades
8pm				▪ Making copies
	Today I gave my practice:	Today I gave my practice:	Today I gave my practice:	▪ Gathering materials
				▪ Other admin tasks (responding to email, positive calls home, etc)
	Tonight I'll give my life:	Tonight I'll give my life:	Tonight I'll give my life:	

Learning Humans

Time	Thursday /	Friday /	Saturday /	Sunday /
6am				
7am				
8am				
9am				
10am				
11am				
12pm				
1pm				
2pm				
3pm				
4pm				
5pm				
6pm				
7pm				
8pm				
	Today I gave my practice: Tonight I'll give my life:	Today I gave my practice: Tonight I'll give my life:	Today I gave my practice: Tonight I'll give my life:	Today I gave my practice: Tonight I'll give my life:

Time	Monday /	Tuesday /	Wednesday /	Guiding Values:
6am				
7am				
8am				
9am				
10am				Interwoven with your general curriculum plans calendar specific times for these activities (selecting times that will minimize your stress):
11am				
12pm				**Own Your Time**
1pm				■ 1 high-value self-care activity/week
2pm				■ 1 work-free hour/day
3pm				■ Which weekend day will be work-free? Circle:
4pm				Saturday Sunday
5pm				**Own Your Classroom:**
6pm				■ Lesson planning (keep this time-bound, or it will take all you give it!)
7pm				■ Evaluating (anything students can't self/peer grade)
8pm				■ Entering grades
	Today I gave my practice: Tonight I'll give my life:	Today I gave my practice: Tonight I'll give my life:	Today I gave my practice: Tonight I'll give my life:	■ Making copies ■ Gathering materials ■ Other admin tasks (responding to email, positive calls home, etc)

Learning Humans

Time	Thursday /	Friday /	Saturday /	Sunday /
6am				
7am				
8am				
9am				
10am				
11am				
12pm				
1pm				
2pm				
3pm				
4pm				
5pm				
6pm				
7pm				
8pm				
	Today I gave my practice: Tonight I'll give my life:	Today I gave my practice: Tonight I'll give my life:	Today I gave my practice: Tonight I'll give my life:	Today I gave my practice: Tonight I'll give my life:

Time	Monday /	Tuesday /	Wednesday /	Guiding Values:
6am				
7am				
8am				
9am				Interwoven with your general curriculum plans calendar specific times for these activities (selecting times that will minimize your stress):
10am				
11am				**Own Your Time**
12pm				▪ 1 high-value self-care activity/week
1pm				▪ 1 work-free hour/day
2pm				▪ Which weekend day will be work-free? Circle: Saturday Sunday
3pm				**Own Your Classroom:**
4pm				▪ Lesson planning (keep this time-bound, or it will take all you give it!)
5pm				▪ Evaluating (anything students can't self/peer grade)
6pm				▪ Entering grades
7pm				▪ Making copies ▪ Gathering materials
8pm				▪ Other admin tasks (responding to email, positive calls home, etc)
	Today I gave my practice: Tonight I'll give my life:	Today I gave my practice: Tonight I'll give my life:	Today I gave my practice: Tonight I'll give my life:	

Learning Humans

Time	Thursday /	Friday /	Saturday /	Sunday /
6am				
7am				
8am				
9am				
10am				
11am				
12pm				
1pm				
2pm				
3pm				
4pm				
5pm				
6pm				
7pm				
8pm				
	Today I gave my practice: Tonight I'll give my life:	Today I gave my practice: Tonight I'll give my life:	Today I gave my practice: Tonight I'll give my life:	Today I gave my practice: Tonight I'll give my life:

Time	Monday /	Tuesday /	Wednesday /	Guiding Values:
6am				
7am				
8am				
9am				Interwoven with your general curriculum plans calendar specific times for these activities (selecting times that will minimize your stress):
10am				
11am				**Own Your Time**
12pm				• 1 high-value self-care activity/week
1pm				• 1 work-free hour/day
2pm				• Which weekend day will be work-free? Circle:
3pm				Saturday Sunday
4pm				**Own Your Classroom:**
5pm				• Lesson planning (keep this time-bound, or it will take all you give it!)
6pm				• Evaluating (anything students can't self/peer grade)
7pm				• Entering grades
				• Making copies
8pm				• Gathering materials
				• Other admin tasks (responding to email, positive calls home, etc)
	Today I gave my practice:	Today I gave my practice:	Today I gave my practice:	
	Tonight I'll give my life:	Tonight I'll give my life:	Tonight I'll give my life:	

Learning Humans

Time	Thursday /	Friday /	Saturday /	Sunday /
6am				
7am				
8am				
9am				
10am				
11am				
12pm				
1pm				
2pm				
3pm				
4pm				
5pm				
6pm				
7pm				
8pm				
	Today I gave my practice: Tonight I'll give my life:	Today I gave my practice: Tonight I'll give my life:	Today I gave my practice: Tonight I'll give my life:	Today I gave my practice: Tonight I'll give my life:

Learning Humans

Time	Monday /	Tuesday /	Wednesday /	**Guiding Values:**
6am				
7am				
8am				
9am				Interwoven with your general curriculum plans calendar specific times for these activities (selecting times that will minimize your stress):
10am				
11am				**Own Your Time**
12pm				• 1 high-value self-care activity/week
1pm				• 1 work-free hour/day • Which weekend day will be work-free? Circle:
2pm				Saturday Sunday
3pm				**Own Your Classroom:** • Lesson planning (keep this time-bound, or it will take all you give it!)
4pm				
5pm				• Evaluating (anything students can't self/peer grade)
6pm				• Entering grades • Making copies
7pm				• Gathering materials • Other admin tasks (responding to email, positive calls home, etc)
8pm				
	Today I gave my practice: Tonight I'll give my life:	Today I gave my practice: Tonight I'll give my life:	Today I gave my practice: Tonight I'll give my life:	

Learning Humans

Time	Thursday /	Friday /	Saturday /	Sunday /
6am				
7am				
8am				
9am				
10am				
11am				
12pm				
1pm				
2pm				
3pm				
4pm				
5pm				
6pm				
7pm				
8pm				
	Today I gave my practice: Tonight I'll give my life:	Today I gave my practice: Tonight I'll give my life:	Today I gave my practice: Tonight I'll give my life:	Today I gave my practice: Tonight I'll give my life:

Time	Monday /	Tuesday /	Wednesday /	Guiding Values:
6am				
7am				
8am				
9am				Interwoven with your general curriculum plans calendar specific times for these activities (selecting times that will minimize your stress):
10am				
11am				**Own Your Time**
12pm				▪ 1 high-value self-care activity/week
1pm				▪ 1 work-free hour/day
2pm				▪ Which weekend day will be work-free? Circle: Saturday Sunday
3pm				**Own Your Classroom:**
4pm				▪ Lesson planning (keep this time-bound, or it will take all you give it!)
5pm				▪ Evaluating (anything students can't self/peer grade)
6pm				▪ Entering grades
7pm				▪ Making copies ▪ Gathering materials
8pm				▪ Other admin tasks (responding to email, positive calls home, etc)
	Today I gave my practice: Tonight I'll give my life:	Today I gave my practice: Tonight I'll give my life:	Today I gave my practice: Tonight I'll give my life:	

Learning Humans

Time	Thursday /	Friday /	Saturday /	Sunday /
6am				
7am				
8am				
9am				
10am				
11am				
12pm				
1pm				
2pm				
3pm				
4pm				
5pm				
6pm				
7pm				
8pm				
	Today I gave my practice:	Today I gave my practice:	Today I gave my practice:	Today I gave my practice:
	Tonight I'll give my life:	Tonight I'll give my life:	Tonight I'll give my life:	Tonight I'll give my life:

Time	Monday /	Tuesday /	Wednesday /	Guiding Values:
6am				
7am				
8am				
9am				Interwoven with your general curriculum plans calendar specific times for these activities (selecting times that will minimize your stress):
10am				
11am				**Own Your Time**
12pm				▪ 1 high-value self-care activity/week
1pm				▪ 1 work-free hour/day
2pm				▪ Which weekend day will be work-free? Circle: Saturday Sunday
3pm				**Own Your Classroom:**
4pm				▪ Lesson planning (keep this time-bound, or it will take all you give it!)
5pm				▪ Evaluating (anything students can't self/peer grade)
6pm				▪ Entering grades
7pm				▪ Making copies ▪ Gathering materials
8pm				▪ Other admin tasks (responding to email, positive calls home, etc)
	Today I gave my practice: Tonight I'll give my life:	Today I gave my practice: Tonight I'll give my life:	Today I gave my practice: Tonight I'll give my life:	

Learning Humans

Time	Thursday /	Friday /	Saturday /	Sunday /
6am				
7am				
8am				
9am				
10am				
11am				
12pm				
1pm				
2pm				
3pm				
4pm				
5pm				
6pm				
7pm				
8pm				
	Today I gave my practice: Tonight I'll give my life:	Today I gave my practice: Tonight I'll give my life:	Today I gave my practice: Tonight I'll give my life:	Today I gave my practice: Tonight I'll give my life:

Learning Humans

Time	Monday /	Tuesday /	Wednesday /	**Guiding Values:**
6am				
7am				
8am				
9am				Interwoven with your general curriculum plans calendar specific times for these activities (selecting times that will minimize your stress):
10am				
11am				**Own Your Time**
12pm				▪ 1 high-value self-care activity/week
1pm				▪ 1 work-free hour/day
2pm				▪ Which weekend day will be work-free? Circle: Saturday Sunday
3pm				**Own Your Classroom:**
4pm				▪ Lesson planning (keep this time-bound, or it will take all you give it!)
5pm				▪ Evaluating (anything students can't self/peer grade)
6pm				▪ Entering grades
7pm				▪ Making copies ▪ Gathering materials
8pm				▪ Other admin tasks (responding to email, positive calls home, etc)
	Today I gave my practice:

Tonight I'll give my life: | Today I gave my practice:

Tonight I'll give my life: | Today I gave my practice:

Tonight I'll give my life: | |

Learning Humans

Time	Thursday /	Friday /	Saturday /	Sunday /
6am				
7am				
8am				
9am				
10am				
11am				
12pm				
1pm				
2pm				
3pm				
4pm				
5pm				
6pm				
7pm				
8pm				
	Today I gave my practice: Tonight I'll give my life:	Today I gave my practice: Tonight I'll give my life:	Today I gave my practice: Tonight I'll give my life:	Today I gave my practice: Tonight I'll give my life:

Time	Monday /	Tuesday /	Wednesday /	Guiding Values:
6am				
7am				
8am				
9am				
10am				
11am				
12pm				
1pm				
2pm				
3pm				
4pm				
5pm				
6pm				
7pm				
8pm				

Interwoven with your general curriculum plans calendar specific times for these activities (selecting times that will minimize your stress):

Own Your Time
- 1 high-value self-care activity/week
- 1 work-free hour/day
- Which weekend day will be work-free?
  Circle:

  Saturday Sunday

Own Your Classroom:
- Lesson planning (keep this time-bound, or it will take all you give it!)
- Evaluating (anything students can't self/peer grade)
- Entering grades
- Making copies
- Gathering materials
- Other admin tasks (responding to email, positive calls home, etc)

Today I gave my practice:

Tonight I'll give my life:

Today I gave my practice:

Tonight I'll give my life:

Today I gave my practice:

Tonight I'll give my life:

Learning Humans

Time	Thursday /	Friday /	Saturday /	Sunday /
6am				
7am				
8am				
9am				
10am				
11am				
12pm				
1pm				
2pm				
3pm				
4pm				
5pm				
6pm				
7pm				
8pm				
	Today I gave my practice: Tonight I'll give my life:	Today I gave my practice: Tonight I'll give my life:	Today I gave my practice: Tonight I'll give my life:	Today I gave my practice: Tonight I'll give my life:

Time	Monday /	Tuesday /	Wednesday /	Guiding Values:
6am				
7am				
8am				
9am				Interwoven with your general curriculum plans calendar specific times for these activities (selecting times that will minimize your stress):
10am				
11am				**Own Your Time** ▪ 1 high-value self-care activity/week
12pm				▪ 1 work-free hour/day
1pm				▪ Which weekend day will be work-free? Circle:
2pm				Saturday Sunday
3pm				**Own Your Classroom:** ▪ Lesson planning (keep this time-bound, or it will take all you give it!)
4pm				
5pm				▪ Evaluating (anything students can't self/peer grade)
6pm				▪ Entering grades ▪ Making copies
7pm				▪ Gathering materials
8pm				▪ Other admin tasks (responding to email, positive calls home, etc)
	Today I gave my practice: Tonight I'll give my life:	Today I gave my practice: Tonight I'll give my life:	Today I gave my practice: Tonight I'll give my life:	

Learning Humans

Time	Thursday /	Friday /	Saturday /	Sunday /
6am				
7am				
8am				
9am				
10am				
11am				
12pm				
1pm				
2pm				
3pm				
4pm				
5pm				
6pm				
7pm				
8pm				
	Today I gave my practice: Tonight I'll give my life:	Today I gave my practice: Tonight I'll give my life:	Today I gave my practice: Tonight I'll give my life:	Today I gave my practice: Tonight I'll give my life:

Learning Humans

Time	Monday /	Tuesday /	Wednesday /	Guiding Values:
6am				
7am				
8am				
9am				Interwoven with your general curriculum plans calendar specific times for these activities (selecting times that will minimize your stress):
10am				
11am				
12pm				**Own Your Time**
1pm				▪ 1 high-value self-care activity/week
2pm				▪ 1 work-free hour/day
3pm				▪ Which weekend day will be work-free? Circle:
4pm				Saturday Sunday
5pm				**Own Your Classroom:**
6pm				▪ Lesson planning (keep this time-bound, or it will take all you give it!)
7pm				▪ Evaluating (anything students can't self/peer grade)
8pm				▪ Entering grades
	Today I gave my practice: Tonight I'll give my life:	Today I gave my practice: Tonight I'll give my life:	Today I gave my practice: Tonight I'll give my life:	▪ Making copies ▪ Gathering materials ▪ Other admin tasks (responding to email, positive calls home, etc)

Learning Humans

Time	Thursday /	Friday /	Saturday /	Sunday /
6am				
7am				
8am				
9am				
10am				
11am				
12pm				
1pm				
2pm				
3pm				
4pm				
5pm				
6pm				
7pm				
8pm				
	Today I gave my practice: Tonight I'll give my life:	Today I gave my practice: Tonight I'll give my life:	Today I gave my practice: Tonight I'll give my life:	Today I gave my practice: Tonight I'll give my life:

Learning Humans

Time	Monday /	Tuesday /	Wednesday /	Guiding Values:
6am				
7am				
8am				
9am				Interwoven with your general curriculum plans calendar specific times for these activities (selecting times that will minimize your stress):
10am				
11am				**Own Your Time**
12pm				▪ 1 high-value self-care activity/week
1pm				▪ 1 work-free hour/day
2pm				▪ Which weekend day will be work-free? Circle: Saturday Sunday
3pm				**Own Your Classroom:**
4pm				▪ Lesson planning (keep this time-bound, or it will take all you give it!)
5pm				▪ Evaluating (anything students can't self/peer grade)
6pm				▪ Entering grades ▪ Making copies
7pm				▪ Gathering materials ▪ Other admin tasks (responding to email, positive calls home, etc)
8pm				
	Today I gave my practice: Tonight I'll give my life:	Today I gave my practice: Tonight I'll give my life:	Today I gave my practice: Tonight I'll give my life:	

Learning Humans

Time	Thursday /	Friday /	Saturday /	Sunday /
6am				
7am				
8am				
9am				
10am				
11am				
12pm				
1pm				
2pm				
3pm				
4pm				
5pm				
6pm				
7pm				
8pm				
	Today I gave my practice: Tonight I'll give my life:	Today I gave my practice: Tonight I'll give my life:	Today I gave my practice: Tonight I'll give my life:	Today I gave my practice: Tonight I'll give my life:

Time	Monday /	Tuesday /	Wednesday /	Guiding Values:
6am				
7am				
8am				
9am				Interwoven with your general curriculum plans calendar specific times for these activities (selecting times that will minimize your stress):
10am				
11am				**Own Your Time**
12pm				▪ 1 high-value self-care activity/week
1pm				▪ 1 work-free hour/day
2pm				▪ Which weekend day will be work-free? Circle: Saturday Sunday
3pm				**Own Your Classroom:**
4pm				▪ Lesson planning (keep this time-bound, or it will take all you give it!)
5pm				▪ Evaluating (anything students can't self/peer grade)
6pm				▪ Entering grades
7pm				▪ Making copies
				▪ Gathering materials
8pm				▪ Other admin tasks (responding to email, positive calls home, etc)
	Today I gave my practice:	Today I gave my practice:	Today I gave my practice:	
	Tonight I'll give my life:	Tonight I'll give my life:	Tonight I'll give my life:	

Learning Humans

Time	Thursday /	Friday /	Saturday /	Sunday /
6am				
7am				
8am				
9am				
10am				
11am				
12pm				
1pm				
2pm				
3pm				
4pm				
5pm				
6pm				
7pm				
8pm				
	Today I gave my practice: Tonight I'll give my life:	Today I gave my practice: Tonight I'll give my life:	Today I gave my practice: Tonight I'll give my life:	Today I gave my practice: Tonight I'll give my life:

Time	Monday /	Tuesday /	Wednesday /	Guiding Values:
6am				
7am				
8am				
9am				Interwoven with your general curriculum plans calendar specific times for these activities (selecting times that will minimize your stress):
10am				
11am				**Own Your Time**
12pm				▪ 1 high-value self-care activity/week
1pm				▪ 1 work-free hour/day
2pm				▪ Which weekend day will be work-free? Circle: Saturday Sunday
3pm				**Own Your Classroom:**
4pm				▪ Lesson planning (keep this time-bound, or it will take all you give it!)
5pm				▪ Evaluating (anything students can't self/peer grade)
6pm				▪ Entering grades
7pm				▪ Making copies
8pm				▪ Gathering materials
	Today I gave my practice: Tonight I'll give my life:	Today I gave my practice: Tonight I'll give my life:	Today I gave my practice: Tonight I'll give my life:	▪ Other admin tasks (responding to email, positive calls home, etc)

Learning Humans

Time	Thursday /	Friday /	Saturday /	Sunday /
6am				
7am				
8am				
9am				
10am				
11am				
12pm				
1pm				
2pm				
3pm				
4pm				
5pm				
6pm				
7pm				
8pm				
	Today I gave my practice:	Today I gave my practice:	Today I gave my practice:	Today I gave my practice:
	Tonight I'll give my life:	Tonight I'll give my life:	Tonight I'll give my life:	Tonight I'll give my life:

Time	Monday /	Tuesday /	Wednesday /	Guiding Values:
6am				
7am				
8am				
9am				Interwoven with your general curriculum plans calendar specific times for these activities (selecting times that will minimize your stress):
10am				
11am				**Own Your Time**
12pm				• 1 high-value self-care activity/week
1pm				• 1 work-free hour/day
				• Which weekend day will be work-free? Circle:
2pm				Saturday Sunday
3pm				**Own Your Classroom:**
4pm				• Lesson planning (keep this time-bound, or it will take all you give it!)
5pm				• Evaluating (anything students can't self/peer grade)
6pm				• Entering grades
				• Making copies
7pm				• Gathering materials
				• Other admin tasks (responding to email, positive calls home, etc)
8pm				
	Today I gave my practice:	Today I gave my practice:	Today I gave my practice:	
	Tonight I'll give my life:	Tonight I'll give my life:	Tonight I'll give my life:	

Learning Humans

Time	Thursday /	Friday /	Saturday /	Sunday /
6am				
7am				
8am				
9am				
10am				
11am				
12pm				
1pm				
2pm				
3pm				
4pm				
5pm				
6pm				
7pm				
8pm				
	Today I gave my practice: Tonight I'll give my life:	Today I gave my practice: Tonight I'll give my life:	Today I gave my practice: Tonight I'll give my life:	Today I gave my practice: Tonight I'll give my life:

Learning Humans

Time	Monday /	Tuesday /	Wednesday /	Guiding Values:
6am				
7am				
8am				
9am				Interwoven with your general curriculum plans calendar specific times for these activities (selecting times that will minimize your stress):
10am				
11am				
12pm				
1pm				
2pm				
3pm				
4pm				
5pm				
6pm				
7pm				
8pm				

Own Your Time
- 1 high-value self-care activity/week
- 1 work-free hour/day
- Which weekend day will be work-free? Circle:

  Saturday Sunday

Own Your Classroom:
- Lesson planning (keep this time-bound, or it will take all you give it!)
- Evaluating (anything students can't self/peer grade)
- Entering grades
- Making copies
- Gathering materials
- Other admin tasks (responding to email, positive calls home, etc)

Monday	Tuesday	Wednesday
Today I gave my practice:	Today I gave my practice:	Today I gave my practice:
Tonight I'll give my life:	Tonight I'll give my life:	Tonight I'll give my life:

Learning Humans

Time	Thursday /	Friday /	Saturday /	Sunday /
6am				
7am				
8am				
9am				
10am				
11am				
12pm				
1pm				
2pm				
3pm				
4pm				
5pm				
6pm				
7pm				
8pm				
	Today I gave my practice: Tonight I'll give my life:	Today I gave my practice: Tonight I'll give my life:	Today I gave my practice: Tonight I'll give my life:	Today I gave my practice: Tonight I'll give my life:

Learning Humans

Time	Monday /	Tuesday /	Wednesday /	Guiding Values:
6am				
7am				
8am				
9am				Interwoven with your general curriculum plans calendar specific times for these activities (selecting times that will minimize your stress):
10am				
11am				**Own Your Time**
12pm				• 1 high-value self-care activity/week
1pm				• 1 work-free hour/day
2pm				• Which weekend day will be work-free? Circle:
3pm				Saturday Sunday
4pm				**Own Your Classroom:**
5pm				• Lesson planning (keep this time-bound, or it will take all you give it!)
6pm				• Evaluating (anything students can't self/peer grade)
7pm				• Entering grades
8pm				• Making copies
				• Gathering materials
	Today I gave my practice:

Tonight I'll give my life: | Today I gave my practice:

Tonight I'll give my life: | Today I gave my practice:

Tonight I'll give my life: | • Other admin tasks (responding to email, positive calls home, etc) |

Learning Humans

Time	Thursday /	Friday /	Saturday /	Sunday /
6am				
7am				
8am				
9am				
10am				
11am				
12pm				
1pm				
2pm				
3pm				
4pm				
5pm				
6pm				
7pm				
8pm				
	Today I gave my practice:	Today I gave my practice:	Today I gave my practice:	Today I gave my practice:
	Tonight I'll give my life:	Tonight I'll give my life:	Tonight I'll give my life:	Tonight I'll give my life:

Learning Humans

Time	Monday /	Tuesday /	Wednesday /	Guiding Values:
6am				
7am				
8am				
9am				Interwoven with your general curriculum plans calendar specific times for these activities (selecting times that will minimize your stress):
10am				
11am				**Own Your Time**
12pm				▪ 1 high-value self-care activity/week
1pm				▪ 1 work-free hour/day ▪ Which weekend day will be work-free? Circle:
2pm				Saturday Sunday
3pm				**Own Your Classroom:** ▪ Lesson planning (keep this time-bound, or it will take all you give it!)
4pm				▪ Evaluating (anything students can't self/peer grade)
5pm				▪ Entering grades
6pm				▪ Making copies ▪ Gathering materials
7pm				▪ Other admin tasks (responding to email, positive calls home, etc)
8pm				
	Today I gave my practice: Tonight I'll give my life:	Today I gave my practice: Tonight I'll give my life:	Today I gave my practice: Tonight I'll give my life:	

🧠 Learning Humans

Time	Thursday /	Friday /	Saturday /	Sunday /
6am				
7am				
8am				
9am				
10am				
11am				
12pm				
1pm				
2pm				
3pm				
4pm				
5pm				
6pm				
7pm				
8pm				
	Today I gave my practice: Tonight I'll give my life:	Today I gave my practice: Tonight I'll give my life:	Today I gave my practice: Tonight I'll give my life:	Today I gave my practice: Tonight I'll give my life:

Time	Monday /	Tuesday /	Wednesday /	Guiding Values:
6am				
7am				
8am				
9am				Interwoven with your general curriculum plans calendar specific times for these activities (selecting times that will minimize your stress):
10am				
11am				**Own Your Time**
12pm				▪ 1 high-value self-care activity/week
1pm				▪ 1 work-free hour/day ▪ Which weekend day will be work-free? Circle:
2pm				Saturday Sunday
3pm				**Own Your Classroom:**
4pm				▪ Lesson planning (keep this time-bound, or it will take all you give it!)
5pm				▪ Evaluating (anything students can't self/peer grade)
6pm				▪ Entering grades ▪ Making copies
7pm				▪ Gathering materials ▪ Other admin tasks (responding to email, positive calls home, etc)
8pm				
	Today I gave my practice: Tonight I'll give my life:	Today I gave my practice: Tonight I'll give my life:	Today I gave my practice: Tonight I'll give my life:	

Learning Humans

Time	Thursday /	Friday /	Saturday /	Sunday /
6am				
7am				
8am				
9am				
10am				
11am				
12pm				
1pm				
2pm				
3pm				
4pm				
5pm				
6pm				
7pm				
8pm				
	Today I gave my practice: Tonight I'll give my life:	Today I gave my practice: Tonight I'll give my life:	Today I gave my practice: Tonight I'll give my life:	Today I gave my practice: Tonight I'll give my life:

Time	Monday /	Tuesday /	Wednesday /	Guiding Values:
6am				
7am				
8am				
9am				Interwoven with your general curriculum plans calendar specific times for these activities (selecting times that will minimize your stress):
10am				
11am				**Own Your Time**
12pm				▪ 1 high-value self-care activity/week
1pm				▪ 1 work-free hour/day
2pm				▪ Which weekend day will be work-free? Circle: Saturday Sunday
3pm				**Own Your Classroom:**
4pm				▪ Lesson planning (keep this time-bound, or it will take all you give it!)
5pm				▪ Evaluating (anything students can't self/peer grade)
6pm				▪ Entering grades
7pm				▪ Making copies ▪ Gathering materials
8pm				▪ Other admin tasks (responding to email, positive calls home, etc)
	Today I gave my practice: Tonight I'll give my life:	Today I gave my practice: Tonight I'll give my life:	Today I gave my practice: Tonight I'll give my life:	

Learning Humans

Time	Thursday /	Friday /	Saturday /	Sunday /
6am				
7am				
8am				
9am				
10am				
11am				
12pm				
1pm				
2pm				
3pm				
4pm				
5pm				
6pm				
7pm				
8pm				
	Today I gave my practice: Tonight I'll give my life:	Today I gave my practice: Tonight I'll give my life:	Today I gave my practice: Tonight I'll give my life:	Today I gave my practice: Tonight I'll give my life:

Time	Monday /	Tuesday /	Wednesday /	Guiding Values:
6am				
7am				
8am				
9am				Interwoven with your general curriculum plans calendar specific times for these activities (selecting times that will minimize your stress):
10am				
11am				**Own Your Time**
12pm				• 1 high-value self-care activity/week
1pm				• 1 work-free hour/day
2pm				• Which weekend day will be work-free? Circle: Saturday Sunday
3pm				**Own Your Classroom:**
4pm				• Lesson planning (keep this time-bound, or it will take all you give it!)
5pm				• Evaluating (anything students can't self/peer grade)
6pm				• Entering grades
7pm				• Making copies
				• Gathering materials
8pm				• Other admin tasks (responding to email, positive calls home, etc)
	Today I gave my practice: Tonight I'll give my life:	Today I gave my practice: Tonight I'll give my life:	Today I gave my practice: Tonight I'll give my life:	

Learning Humans

Time	Thursday /	Friday /	Saturday /	Sunday /
6am				
7am				
8am				
9am				
10am				
11am				
12pm				
1pm				
2pm				
3pm				
4pm				
5pm				
6pm				
7pm				
8pm				
	Today I gave my practice: Tonight I'll give my life:	Today I gave my practice: Tonight I'll give my life:	Today I gave my practice: Tonight I'll give my life:	Today I gave my practice: Tonight I'll give my life:

Learning Humans

Time	Monday /	Tuesday /	Wednesday /	**Guiding Values:**
6am				
7am				
8am				
9am				Interwoven with your general curriculum plans calendar specific times for these activities (selecting times that will minimize your stress):
10am				
11am				**Own Your Time**
12pm				▪ 1 high-value self-care activity/week
1pm				▪ 1 work-free hour/day
2pm				▪ Which weekend day will be work-free? Circle:
3pm				Saturday Sunday
4pm				**Own Your Classroom:**
5pm				▪ Lesson planning (keep this time-bound, or it will take all you give it!)
6pm				▪ Evaluating (anything students can't self/peer grade)
7pm				▪ Entering grades
8pm				▪ Making copies
	Today I gave my practice: Tonight I'll give my life:	Today I gave my practice: Tonight I'll give my life:	Today I gave my practice: Tonight I'll give my life:	▪ Gathering materials ▪ Other admin tasks (responding to email, positive calls home, etc)

Learning Humans

Time	Thursday /	Friday /	Saturday /	Sunday /
6am				
7am				
8am				
9am				
10am				
11am				
12pm				
1pm				
2pm				
3pm				
4pm				
5pm				
6pm				
7pm				
8pm				
	Today I gave my practice: Tonight I'll give my life:	Today I gave my practice: Tonight I'll give my life:	Today I gave my practice: Tonight I'll give my life:	Today I gave my practice: Tonight I'll give my life:

Time	Monday /	Tuesday /	Wednesday /	Guiding Values:
6am				
7am				
8am				
9am				Interwoven with your general curriculum plans calendar specific times for these activities (selecting times that will minimize your stress):
10am				
11am				**Own Your Time**
12pm				▪ 1 high-value self-care activity/week
1pm				▪ 1 work-free hour/day
2pm				▪ Which weekend day will be work-free? Circle: Saturday Sunday
3pm				**Own Your Classroom:**
4pm				▪ Lesson planning (keep this time-bound, or it will take all you give it!)
5pm				▪ Evaluating (anything students can't self/peer grade)
6pm				▪ Entering grades
7pm				▪ Making copies ▪ Gathering materials ▪ Other admin tasks (responding to email, positive calls home, etc)
8pm				
	Today I gave my practice: Tonight I'll give my life:	Today I gave my practice: Tonight I'll give my life:	Today I gave my practice: Tonight I'll give my life:	

Learning Humans

Time	Thursday /	Friday /	Saturday /	Sunday /
6am				
7am				
8am				
9am				
10am				
11am				
12pm				
1pm				
2pm				
3pm				
4pm				
5pm				
6pm				
7pm				
8pm				
	Today I gave my practice: Tonight I'll give my life:	Today I gave my practice: Tonight I'll give my life:	Today I gave my practice: Tonight I'll give my life:	Today I gave my practice: Tonight I'll give my life:

Time	Monday /	Tuesday /	Wednesday /	Guiding Values:
6am				
7am				
8am				
9am				Interwoven with your general curriculum plans calendar specific times for these activities (selecting times that will minimize your stress):
10am				
11am				**Own Your Time**
12pm				▪ 1 high-value self-care activity/week
1pm				▪ 1 work-free hour/day
2pm				▪ Which weekend day will be work-free? Circle: Saturday Sunday
3pm				**Own Your Classroom:**
4pm				▪ Lesson planning (keep this time-bound, or it will take all you give it!)
5pm				▪ Evaluating (anything students can't self/peer grade)
6pm				▪ Entering grades
7pm				▪ Making copies ▪ Gathering materials
8pm				▪ Other admin tasks (responding to email, positive calls home, etc)
	Today I gave my practice: Tonight I'll give my life:	Today I gave my practice: Tonight I'll give my life:	Today I gave my practice: Tonight I'll give my life:	

Learning Humans

Time	Thursday /	Friday /	Saturday /	Sunday /
6am				
7am				
8am				
9am				
10am				
11am				
12pm				
1pm				
2pm				
3pm				
4pm				
5pm				
6pm				
7pm				
8pm				
	Today I gave my practice: Tonight I'll give my life:	Today I gave my practice: Tonight I'll give my life:	Today I gave my practice: Tonight I'll give my life:	Today I gave my practice: Tonight I'll give my life:

Learning Humans

Time	Monday /	Tuesday /	Wednesday /	Guiding Values:
6am				
7am				
8am				
9am				Interwoven with your general curriculum plans calendar specific times for these activities (selecting times that will minimize your stress):
10am				
11am				**Own Your Time**
12pm				■ 1 high-value self-care activity/week
1pm				■ 1 work-free hour/day ■ Which weekend day will be work-free? Circle:
2pm				Saturday Sunday
3pm				**Own Your Classroom:** ■ Lesson planning (keep this time-bound, or it will take all you give it!)
4pm				
5pm				■ Evaluating (anything students can't self/peer grade)
6pm				■ Entering grades ■ Making copies
7pm				■ Gathering materials ■ Other admin tasks (responding to email, positive calls home, etc)
8pm				
	Today I gave my practice: Tonight I'll give my life:	Today I gave my practice: Tonight I'll give my life:	Today I gave my practice: Tonight I'll give my life:	

Learning Humans

Time	Thursday /	Friday /	Saturday /	Sunday /
6am				
7am				
8am				
9am				
10am				
11am				
12pm				
1pm				
2pm				
3pm				
4pm				
5pm				
6pm				
7pm				
8pm				
	Today I gave my practice: Tonight I'll give my life:	Today I gave my practice: Tonight I'll give my life:	Today I gave my practice: Tonight I'll give my life:	Today I gave my practice: Tonight I'll give my life:

Time	Monday /	Tuesday /	Wednesday /	Guiding Values:
6am				
7am				
8am				
9am				Interwoven with your general curriculum plans calendar specific times for these activities (selecting times that will minimize your stress):
10am				
11am				**Own Your Time**
12pm				■ 1 high-value self-care activity/week
1pm				■ 1 work-free hour/day
2pm				■ Which weekend day will be work-free? Circle: Saturday Sunday
3pm				**Own Your Classroom:**
4pm				■ Lesson planning (keep this time-bound, or it will take all you give it!)
5pm				■ Evaluating (anything students can't self/peer grade)
6pm				■ Entering grades
7pm				■ Making copies ■ Gathering materials ■ Other admin tasks (responding to email, positive calls home, etc)
8pm				
	Today I gave my practice:	Today I gave my practice:	Today I gave my practice:	
	Tonight I'll give my life:	Tonight I'll give my life:	Tonight I'll give my life:	

🧠 Learning Humans

Time	Thursday /	Friday /	Saturday /	Sunday /
6am				
7am				
8am				
9am				
10am				
11am				
12pm				
1pm				
2pm				
3pm				
4pm				
5pm				
6pm				
7pm				
8pm				
	Today I gave my practice: Tonight I'll give my life:	Today I gave my practice: Tonight I'll give my life:	Today I gave my practice: Tonight I'll give my life:	Today I gave my practice: Tonight I'll give my life:

Time	Monday /	Tuesday /	Wednesday /	Guiding Values:
6am				
7am				
8am				
9am				Interwoven with your general curriculum plans calendar specific times for these activities (selecting times that will minimize your stress):
10am				
11am				**Own Your Time**
12pm				▪ 1 high-value self-care activity/week
1pm				▪ 1 work-free hour/day
2pm				▪ Which weekend day will be work-free? Circle: Saturday Sunday
3pm				**Own Your Classroom:**
4pm				▪ Lesson planning (keep this time-bound, or it will take all you give it!)
5pm				▪ Evaluating (anything students can't self/peer grade)
6pm				▪ Entering grades
7pm				▪ Making copies ▪ Gathering materials
8pm				▪ Other admin tasks (responding to email, positive calls home, etc)
	Today I gave my practice: Tonight I'll give my life:	Today I gave my practice: Tonight I'll give my life:	Today I gave my practice: Tonight I'll give my life:	

Learning Humans

Time	Thursday /	Friday /	Saturday /	Sunday /
6am				
7am				
8am				
9am				
10am				
11am				
12pm				
1pm				
2pm				
3pm				
4pm				
5pm				
6pm				
7pm				
8pm				
	Today I gave my practice: Tonight I'll give my life:	Today I gave my practice: Tonight I'll give my life:	Today I gave my practice: Tonight I'll give my life:	Today I gave my practice: Tonight I'll give my life:

Time	Monday /	Tuesday /	Wednesday /	Guiding Values:
6am				
7am				
8am				
9am				Interwoven with your general curriculum plans calendar specific times for these activities (selecting times that will minimize your stress):
10am				
11am				**Own Your Time**
12pm				▪ 1 high-value self-care activity/week
1pm				▪ 1 work-free hour/day ▪ Which weekend day will be work-free? Circle:
2pm				Saturday Sunday
3pm				**Own Your Classroom:** ▪ Lesson planning (keep this time-bound, or it will take all you give it!)
4pm				
5pm				▪ Evaluating (anything students can't self/peer grade)
6pm				▪ Entering grades ▪ Making copies ▪ Gathering materials
7pm				▪ Other admin tasks (responding to email, positive calls home, etc)
8pm				
	Today I gave my practice: Tonight I'll give my life:	Today I gave my practice: Tonight I'll give my life:	Today I gave my practice: Tonight I'll give my life:	

Learning Humans

Time	Thursday /	Friday /	Saturday /	Sunday /
6am				
7am				
8am				
9am				
10am				
11am				
12pm				
1pm				
2pm				
3pm				
4pm				
5pm				
6pm				
7pm				
8pm				
	Today I gave my practice: Tonight I'll give my life:	Today I gave my practice: Tonight I'll give my life:	Today I gave my practice: Tonight I'll give my life:	Today I gave my practice: Tonight I'll give my life:

Learning Humans

Time	Monday /	Tuesday /	Wednesday /	Guiding Values:
6am				
7am				
8am				
9am				Interwoven with your general curriculum plans calendar specific times for these activities (selecting times that will minimize your stress):
10am				
11am				**Own Your Time**
12pm				▪ 1 high-value self-care activity/week
1pm				▪ 1 work-free hour/day
2pm				▪ Which weekend day will be work-free? Circle: Saturday Sunday
3pm				**Own Your Classroom:**
4pm				▪ Lesson planning (keep this time-bound, or it will take all you give it!)
5pm				▪ Evaluating (anything students can't self/peer grade)
6pm				▪ Entering grades
7pm				▪ Making copies ▪ Gathering materials
8pm				▪ Other admin tasks (responding to email, positive calls home, etc)
	Today I gave my practice: Tonight I'll give my life:	Today I gave my practice: Tonight I'll give my life:	Today I gave my practice: Tonight I'll give my life:	

Learning Humans

Time	Thursday /	Friday /	Saturday /	Sunday /
6am				
7am				
8am				
9am				
10am				
11am				
12pm				
1pm				
2pm				
3pm				
4pm				
5pm				
6pm				
7pm				
8pm				
	Today I gave my practice: Tonight I'll give my life:	Today I gave my practice: Tonight I'll give my life:	Today I gave my practice: Tonight I'll give my life:	Today I gave my practice: Tonight I'll give my life:

Time	Monday /	Tuesday /	Wednesday /	Guiding Values:
6am				
7am				
8am				
9am				Interwoven with your general curriculum plans calendar specific times for these activities (selecting times that will minimize your stress):
10am				
11am				
12pm				
1pm				
2pm				
3pm				
4pm				
5pm				
6pm				
7pm				
8pm				

Own Your Time
- 1 high-value self-care activity/week
- 1 work-free hour/day
- Which weekend day will be work-free? Circle:

  Saturday Sunday

Own Your Classroom:
- Lesson planning (keep this time-bound, or it will take all you give it!)
- Evaluating (anything students can't self/peer grade)
- Entering grades
- Making copies
- Gathering materials
- Other admin tasks (responding to email, positive calls home, etc)

Monday	Tuesday	Wednesday
Today I gave my practice:	Today I gave my practice:	Today I gave my practice:
Tonight I'll give my life:	Tonight I'll give my life:	Tonight I'll give my life:

🧠 Learning Humans

Time	Thursday /	Friday /	Saturday /	Sunday /
6am				
7am				
8am				
9am				
10am				
11am				
12pm				
1pm				
2pm				
3pm				
4pm				
5pm				
6pm				
7pm				
8pm				
	Today I gave my practice: Tonight I'll give my life:	Today I gave my practice: Tonight I'll give my life:	Today I gave my practice: Tonight I'll give my life:	Today I gave my practice: Tonight I'll give my life:

Learning Humans

Time	Monday /	Tuesday /	Wednesday /	Guiding Values:
6am				
7am				
8am				
9am				Interwoven with your general curriculum plans calendar specific times for these activities (selecting times that will minimize your stress):
10am				
11am				**Own Your Time**
12pm				■ 1 high-value self-care activity/week
1pm				■ 1 work-free hour/day ■ Which weekend day will be work-free? Circle: Saturday Sunday
2pm				
3pm				**Own Your Classroom:** ■ Lesson planning (keep this time-bound, or it will take all you give it!)
4pm				
5pm				■ Evaluating (anything students can't self/peer grade)
6pm				■ Entering grades ■ Making copies
7pm				■ Gathering materials ■ Other admin tasks (responding to email, positive calls home, etc)
8pm				
	Today I gave my practice: Tonight I'll give my life:	Today I gave my practice: Tonight I'll give my life:	Today I gave my practice: Tonight I'll give my life:	

Learning Humans

Time	Thursday /	Friday /	Saturday /	Sunday /
6am				
7am				
8am				
9am				
10am				
11am				
12pm				
1pm				
2pm				
3pm				
4pm				
5pm				
6pm				
7pm				
8pm				
	Today I gave my practice: Tonight I'll give my life:	Today I gave my practice: Tonight I'll give my life:	Today I gave my practice: Tonight I'll give my life:	Today I gave my practice: Tonight I'll give my life:

Time	Monday /	Tuesday /	Wednesday /	Guiding Values:
6am				
7am				
8am				
9am				Interwoven with your general curriculum plans calendar specific times for these activities (selecting times that will minimize your stress):
10am				
11am				**Own Your Time** ■ 1 high-value self-care activity/week
12pm				■ 1 work-free hour/day
1pm				■ Which weekend day will be work-free? Circle:
2pm				Saturday Sunday
3pm				**Own Your Classroom:** ■ Lesson planning (keep this time-bound, or it will take all you give it!)
4pm				■ Evaluating (anything students can't self/peer grade)
5pm				■ Entering grades
6pm				■ Making copies ■ Gathering materials
7pm				■ Other admin tasks (responding to email, positive calls home, etc)
8pm				
	Today I gave my practice: Tonight I'll give my life:	Today I gave my practice: Tonight I'll give my life:	Today I gave my practice: Tonight I'll give my life:	

Learning Humans

Time	Thursday /	Friday /	Saturday /	Sunday /
6am				
7am				
8am				
9am				
10am				
11am				
12pm				
1pm				
2pm				
3pm				
4pm				
5pm				
6pm				
7pm				
8pm				
	Today I gave my practice: Tonight I'll give my life:	Today I gave my practice: Tonight I'll give my life:	Today I gave my practice: Tonight I'll give my life:	Today I gave my practice: Tonight I'll give my life:

Learning Humans

Time	Monday /	Tuesday /	Wednesday /	Guiding Values:
6am				
7am				
8am				
9am				Interwoven with your general curriculum plans calendar specific times for these activities (selecting times that will minimize your stress):
10am				
11am				**Own Your Time**
12pm				▪ 1 high-value self-care activity/week
1pm				▪ 1 work-free hour/day
2pm				▪ Which weekend day will be work-free? Circle:
3pm				Saturday Sunday
4pm				**Own Your Classroom:**
5pm				▪ Lesson planning (keep this time-bound, or it will take all you give it!)
6pm				▪ Evaluating (anything students can't self/peer grade)
7pm				▪ Entering grades
8pm				▪ Making copies
	Today I gave my practice:	Today I gave my practice:	Today I gave my practice:	▪ Gathering materials
	Tonight I'll give my life:	Tonight I'll give my life:	Tonight I'll give my life:	▪ Other admin tasks (responding to email, positive calls home, etc)

Learning Humans

Time	Thursday /	Friday /	Saturday /	Sunday /
6am				
7am				
8am				
9am				
10am				
11am				
12pm				
1pm				
2pm				
3pm				
4pm				
5pm				
6pm				
7pm				
8pm				
	Today I gave my practice: Tonight I'll give my life:	Today I gave my practice: Tonight I'll give my life:	Today I gave my practice: Tonight I'll give my life:	Today I gave my practice: Tonight I'll give my life:

Time	Monday /	Tuesday /	Wednesday /	Guiding Values:
6am				
7am				
8am				
9am				Interwoven with your general curriculum plans calendar specific times for these activities (selecting times that will minimize your stress):
10am				
11am				**Own Your Time**
12pm				■ 1 high-value self-care activity/week
1pm				■ 1 work-free hour/day
2pm				■ Which weekend day will be work-free? Circle: Saturday Sunday
3pm				**Own Your Classroom:**
4pm				■ Lesson planning (keep this time-bound, or it will take all you give it!)
5pm				■ Evaluating (anything students can't self/peer grade)
6pm				■ Entering grades
				■ Making copies
7pm				■ Gathering materials
8pm				■ Other admin tasks (responding to email, positive calls home, etc)
	Today I gave my practice: Tonight I'll give my life:	Today I gave my practice: Tonight I'll give my life:	Today I gave my practice: Tonight I'll give my life:	

Learning Humans

Time	Thursday /	Friday /	Saturday /	Sunday /
6am				
7am				
8am				
9am				
10am				
11am				
12pm				
1pm				
2pm				
3pm				
4pm				
5pm				
6pm				
7pm				
8pm				
	Today I gave my practice: Tonight I'll give my life:	Today I gave my practice: Tonight I'll give my life:	Today I gave my practice: Tonight I'll give my life:	Today I gave my practice: Tonight I'll give my life:

Focus		Summer Ideas/Opportunities	Dates	Priority		
PersonaĀ	PersonaĀ			High	Medium	Low

Focus		Summer Ideas/Opportunities	Dates	Priority		
PersonaĀ	PersonaĀ			High	Medium	Low

Learning Humans